Safari Sketchbook

A Bird Painter's African Odyssey

Safari Sketchbook

A Bird Painter's African Odyssey

Martin Woodcock

THE ESKER PRESS

For Barbara, who made things work, and made it fun

The newcomer

I often dreamed that I might stand
on some remote and sun-kissed plain
where bright birds flew, and wild creatures
roamed – but when the dream-flight came at last,
how long it seemed, as in the dark
my long-imagined land crept slowly past.
A glimmer in the eastern sky, and then
a fiery dawn had sparked a blaze
of expectation, which soon cooled, then drowned
in sheeting rain, and violence of the storm.

I waited while the downpour veiled the land,
and waited on impatiently, being new.
Later, the hot earth rose refreshed,
shook its green, wet-heavy mantle at the sun
and sighed, exhaled a breath of virgin wilderness
untamed, as if to cast a spell.
A pace or two along the wet, red murram road
an omen lay – a bird – his wings outspread,
all turquoise, black and red, dead in his glory,
and in the mud revealed the frailty of beauty
in a wild, sun-kissed world.

Published in 2010 by
The Esker Press,
Furlongs,
Long Lane,
Wiveton,
Norfolk NR25 7DD

www.martinwoodcock.co.uk

ISBN 978-0-9564016-0-1

A CIP catalogue record for this book is available from the British Library

Designed by Fluke Art, Cornwall

10 9 8 7 6 5 4 3 2 1

Contents

Foreword
by Field Marshal Sir John Chapple

I first came across Martin Woodcock when the new *Field Guide to the Birds of South-east Asia* appeared in 1975. The illustrations were so accurate and easy to use. The new field guide was also a blessed relief. I used to carry in my pack the very heavy *Birds of Borneo,* by Bertram Smythies. I have to confess that I bought two copies of the new book, and then took all the illustrations out of one copy to carry in my pocket. It was never easy birdwatching whilst on operations in the jungle. If you were sitting in ambush, you couldn't move, and the bird was always 'just over there'. If you were patrolling, you couldn't let your eyes stray to gaze at some new bird sitting in the branches above. Many new field guides have appeared since those days, but these early guides made identification much easier, for which I was grateful to both authors and illustrator.

Then in the early 80s, the *Birds of Africa* project started, and continued for another twenty years, during all of which Martin was heavily engaged in preparing and providing the illustrations. I could not understand how he managed to cover such an enormous number of species. This book – *Safari Sketchbook* – tells us something about how this major task was so successfully tackled.

I have been very fortunate to have visited many corners of the world during my time in the Army. On these official visits I have usually managed to find a few hours to do a bit of birdwatching. My hosts were probably quite glad to get rid of me for a while. They invariably provided me with expert guides as well as transport to get me to the known 'hotspots'. These visits, as well as a few holidays, have taken me to most of the countries in southern and eastern Africa – and I have visited, albeit briefly, some of the places covered in this book.

When I read through the draft text, and looked at the drawings and paintings, I was immediately reminded of the marvellous Hodgson drawings. Brian Houghton Hodgson lived for many years in Nepal, where he collected an amazing number of specimens. These are now mostly in the Natural History Museum. He also made copious notes, and many of these are in the Linnean Society. His volumes of drawings and paintings are in the library of the Zoological Society of London. They are covered with notes in English and Nagri describing where the bird was seen, or where the specimen had been collected. Martin's fascinating notes and drawings brought back vividly for the first time the youthful memories of looking through Hodgson's drawings, which had made such an impression on me.

I am very envious of Martin and Barbara's adventurous fieldwork – some of it very hard, but so rewarding and at times such fun. Martin's art brings the birds alive. This Odyssey brings the artist alive.

John Chapple

Preface

It comes almost as a shock, to see the electric-blue flash of the speeding kingfisher under a grey English sky. It is purely visual, as bright a thing as you will see with birds – as bright as anything in the tropics. The steely glint of the first swallow, though, searching for insects over the brown reeds on a cold spring day, is wonderfully thought-provoking.

Year after year, but in a moment, too, it evokes all the wonder about how birds live, and what can power and motivate such a seemingly fragile scrap of feathers to migrate. Gilbert White, in the eighteenth century, may have suspected that swallows migrated, perhaps even had a shrewd idea of where they went, but even he would have been astounded to learn that the pair nesting in his shed were the same birds as the year before, and had in the meantime flown twice across Africa. I had a chance, in my twenties, to go where Gilbert White's swallows went, to see the places that were as familiar to them as Selborne, and the birds and animals that they knew well, but that I had seen only in the zoo.

The nearest thing to birdwatching in the tropics for me had been in the heat of summer in the Camargue, where distant flamingos shimmered in a haze of mosquitos, the black bulls imagined they were buffalos, and bee-eaters, whose beautiful but rather static portrait by Thorburn I had admired since childhood, were wonderfully aerial and vocal in the hot sky. Now I was to be dealt a pack of the brightest, most diverse images that I could ever have imagined, though of course, at the back of my mind, I had been half-hoping for something like this, not knowing how it would really be.

I was soon to find out. I was sitting in the back seat of a Volkswagen 'Beetle' driven by my sister, bumping slowly along a track in Uganda. On our left, a big thorny bush stood by the track, and, as we eased past it, there stood a massive bull elephant, gently flapping his ears, the tip of his trunk touching the car. He was wider across the head and ears than the length of the car, and I looked up in total awe and severe apprehension, and slid down instinctively into the well behind the front seats. A month in Uganda and I was well and truly hooked – into Africa and practically out of my mind – and there followed a brief but determined excursion through Kenya to the Ngorongoro crater, with the 'Beetle' sailing imperiously through floodwater on its tin-tray chassis.

Several trips, and many years later, another chance came. One day in 1978, quite unexpectedly, I received a letter from Academic Press in London, to say that they were contemplating publishing a major work on African birds, which would be fully illustrated. Leslie Brown who, with Emil Urban was the project's godfather, had seen illustrations of mine in the *Field Guide to the Birds of South-east Asia*, and had suggested my name to the publishers in case I could contribute. There were to be four volumes, and two other illustrators had been engaged.

Red-throated Bee-eaters.

After I had painted some plates of gamebirds and shorebirds, originally destined for volume 1, it became clear that there had been some problems and delays, and also that, like Big Bang at an early stage, the whole project had undergone a rapid and virtually uncontrolled expansion. I was invited to lunch by the publishers with Leslie Brown and Emil Urban to discuss this development, and Leslie, anxious to keep the project on the rails, suddenly suggested that he would prefer just one illustrator, and that it should be me.

I probably gulped – Emil says he will always remember my face as Leslie spoke. A huge feeling of inadequacy settled on me. This suggestion needed some serious thought. It would be a huge task, with the work now expected to extend to five volumes, and I would need to know a great deal more about African birds in the field. After a week or so, I nervously agreed to the proposition, but none of us knew then that Leslie would shortly be dead, that the editorial team would expand, and that the number of volumes, five by now, would need to grow to six, and then seven. The timescale stretched like elastic, and it would be more than twenty years before the final volume was completed.

For a couple of years I had to carry on painting from museum skins, and had completed most of the plates for the first three volumes. Then, with the four volumes of passerines looming, field-work in Africa became a priority. This was made immeasurably easier as Neil Baker, a birder living in Tanzania, had offered help with the project, and, after enthusing various of his friends and colleagues, an initial four month trip became a real possibility. Kenya, Tanzania and South Africa were the focus this time, and on several subsequent trips, but later on I was able to study birds in other parts of Africa as well. The field studies became an end in themselves, as it rapidly became clear that it would be impossible to concentrate exclusively on passerines. Although I made every effort in this connection, a much greater variety of work resulted on some of the trips, mostly between 1983 and 1995, which I have been able to use in this book, and the text is derived from my journals.

However, for every sketch, for every notebook entry, there are a thousand mental images – images that could never make it on to paper. I still see that tiny cisticola, dancing in the clouds, and the white-winged terns, in their hundreds of thousands by Lake Manyara – like splinters of light in the white heat haze, twisting, turning and fading in a horizonless shimmering mirage. On the shore, in stark contrast, those brutes of birds – the marabous – stalked stiffly about, wielding their massive beaks. How does one catch the flashing to and fro of sunbirds at flowering *Leonotis,* or the jostling football crowd of vultures at a carcass?

We are privileged that there are still so many wonderful things to see, and so much still to learn, and all of us must shoulder the responsibility for preserving this treasure we have inherited for future generations.

Despite many trips, I still feel that I have barely scratched the surface; unlimited time and resources and a greater skill would have been nice. Many compromises had to be made, but even allowing for that, it was a once in a lifetime experience, and given a chance, I would gladly do it again. As Mae West remarked, too much of a good thing is just wonderful.

Note. Some of the English names on the sketch-pages are not those currently in use. To avoid ambiguity, the names in the text and captions are those recommended by the African Bird Club in its Checklist of African Birds, 2009. To give metric in addition to Imperial measurements seems unsuitable in this kind of book, so I have decided to follow my practice in the journals, and use Imperial in the text.

First impressions — Uganda 1961

Dawn had been sublime, as the sun rose in a great glory over the desert near Khartoum; what had been a mysterious dark serpentine line below, turned brilliant green where the narrow Nile valley wound away into the misty morning, southwards in the Sudan. As we came in to land at Entebbe, though, it was as grey and cloudy as an English morning, and a violent rainstorm was lashing the lake.

My notebook was in action before the plane doors had opened, but there was a long wait before I stepped out onto a hot and humid green land, with a truly tropical smell that hinted at spices, flowering shrubs, damp earth and I know not what else. Abdim's Storks walked about along the landing strip, Hooded Vultures and Black Kites circled around, and Common Fiscal Shrikes perched everywhere along wires and fences. The kingfisher I was used to – small and dumpy, and always a waterside bird – was here transformed into a larger bird of bush and gardens, and before I had taken ten steps on the red earth, I saw one lying dead on the ground. It seemed to epitomise in one striking image both the beauty and the fragility of life here – the indifference of nature to its own creation coming almost as a shock. I picked the bird up and later drew it, and so a dead bird became the sketchbook's first entry in years of trying to capture the life of Africa's birds.

My sister's garden, in a quiet Kampala suburb, was a haven for birds. Listening to the singing bulbuls and the fluty duetting of the Black-headed Gonoleks (black-and-crimson shrikes hiding in the undergrowth), I was drenched in the almost overpowering perfume of the frangipanis, not to mention the perspiration. All of a sudden, when I spotted a Wood Warbler in a bush, I was magically transported back to the fresh leafy spring of an oak-wood in Sussex; my mind raced as I imagined its recent journey here, and thought of how far we had been flown over the desert, following the Nile, as it slithered sinuously for hours like a green snake in the sand.

Everywhere we went there were new birds and, one evening, a walk in the Kitante valley was memorable in a different way. The big fruit bats, the flying foxes, roosted in a belt of gum trees in a wooded part of this lovely park-like valley, and at dusk they flew out, thousands upon thousands – flapping floppily like Lapwings – off to their feeding grounds by the lake. They left their roost in a stream about 200 yards wide, cutting a flickering swathe across the sky, passing for about a quarter of an hour. That evening we also watched the local human residents catching the grasshoppers – 'dudus' – that were swarming around the street lamps, picking them up off the ground, and stuffing them into cans and bags. Fried, they are good to eat, and taste a bit like whitebait.

The Common Bulbul (*above*) may be the commonest bird in all Africa.

Red-throated Bee-eaters.
Paraa   27 December.

Christmas in Kampala was somewhat unreal, since there was a smart Blue-headed Wagtail running about on the lawn, and the Wood Warbler was new for my Christmas day list. Then, early on Boxing Day, we left for the Murchison Falls, with a further mixture of familiar birds amongst the others – wheatears, Marsh Sandpipers and Spur-winged Plovers, rollers and the African Pied Wagtail – an even more boldly marked bird than our own Pied Wagtail. At dusk, I saw a Marabou Stork standing, silhouetted, on one leg on its nest, like some grotesque Arthur Rackham drawing.

The first morning at Paraa Lodge I was out at dawn, but there was a thick mist, and I failed to see an elephant until I was uncomfortably close, and immediately remembered that there were creatures other than birds here. I was quite subdued for a bit. The launch trip up the Nile to the falls was one of the most memorable days I had ever spent; crocodiles teemed along the banks, sliding into the water in shoals as we approached, elephants and buffalo were everywhere, and the birds came so thick and fast I had trouble keeping up with my notes. The Red-throated Bee-eaters nested along the river banks in their hundreds, and there was a constant coming and going of bright green and red birds. Pratincoles and, even better, Skimmers sat on sand-banks, and there were plenty of waders, gulls and herons to list.

A few days in the Queen Elizabeth National Park meant more and more birds and animals, especially along the wonderful Kazinga channel. Along the sandy banks were hundreds of pelicans, marabous, cormorants and Egyptian Geese, clustering in groups, or walking about sedately amongst each other like guests at a reception. Yellow Wagtails and Common Sandpipers ran around – and on – the hippos, and Greenshanks fed by the crocodiles. In one place there were multitudes of European Swallows feeding over grassland, as far as the eye could see, flying over and through the herds of zebra and antelopes that grazed quietly, dotting the plain as I imagined bison used to do in Nebraska. It was a paradise – a scene from the days before man appeared on earth – and I couldn't help feeling that the sheer numbers of swallows suggested that this, rather than our dairy pastures in England, was their real home. I could not even begin to guess their numbers, but a million wouldn't have surprised me at all, and the next few days disclosed more huge flocks, especially around Ishasha.

Red-throated Bee-eaters (*above*) nested in their hundreds along the banks of the Victoria Nile near the Murchison Falls, and there was constant activity with the birds coming and going, or perching on roots in the bank.

10

A complete contrast to these game-rich savannas, and another memorable experience, came when we went to stay with that wonderful and famous little Italian, Toni Nuti, at Kikagati, on her private island of six-and-a-half acres on the Kagera river. She was a feisty and irrepressible character, who had lived in Uganda for many years, spoke several local dialects, and had been accepted into one of the tribes. Various orphaned animals were brought to her for safekeeping, and lived happily on the island – a little reedbuck was very attached to her old golden retriever, and they would wander around together. There was another resident character – Nelson, her favourite hippo. He was allowed into the garden because she knew – and he knew – that, when he had eaten enough, it was indicated to him by the very loud banging of a huge copper saucepan, whereupon he would dutifully retreat into the river. The heavy moist green vegetation and big trees, and the foaming white waters made an unforgettable backdrop to birding around here, and the cooking was of a standard to match. Hippo (though of course not Nelson) was amongst other delicacies on the menu.

The drive from Kampala to Nairobi meant leaving what seemed like a humid, lush garden and entering a much wider and drier landscape. The road was a track, which was no barrier to animals; giraffe and zebra wandered across at all times, and now and again a Secretary Bird would stalk along near the car. A new European bird for me from my window in the

New Stanley hotel was a Pied Wheatear, but it was only a night stop in Nairobi before heading south to Namanga and then the Ngorongoro crater. Owing to the recent heavy rains, the Athi river was flowing over, rather than under, the road bridge, which was evidently damaged, and we spent four hours in a human chain, passing each other rocks to fill in the gaps. It was still under water when we inched over it, and you couldn't see where the sides of the bridge were. At a very grotty small hotel in Namanga I needed to have a bath, and watched impatiently as the deep brown water trickled slowly in, making a sort of buzzing noise. At last I was able to lie back comfortably. I looked up, and saw a huge, busy hornet's nest on the naked light fitting immediately overhead, and jumped out, pretty much like Zebedee going up on a spring, having exchanged a thin layer of perspiration for a thicker layer of mud. A week later, on the way back, the water had fallen 20 feet, and the parapets on the bridge were still missing.

Red-tailed Chat

The dainty little Black-shouldered Kite (*above*) often flicks its tail up, then lets it drop slowly, while the wings are drooped.

The Familiar Chat (*left*) is an unassuming little bird, a bit like a female Common Redstart. A pair was nesting in a shed on Toni Nuti's island, often fluttering down to the ground to pick up an insect.

Owing to the rains, the open, rolling steppe country we drove through after leaving Arusha on the way to the crater was covered with lush green grass, and was absolutely humming with insects. There were huge flocks of Abdim's Storks on these plains, running into many thousands of birds, and also three large separate flocks of Marabous – each of 600 or 700 birds. There were plovers, Spur-winged Geese, Ostriches, Secretary Birds and many others in abundance. In retrospect, this was the greenest I have ever seen this area; on several occasions, many years later, the plain was a pulsating brown mirage, with not a blade of grass in sight.

Golden-winged sunbird in forest on the rim of the crater

My first view of the beautiful Golden-winged Sunbird (*above*) was among dripping fronds of moss in the cloud-hung forest on the crater's rim.

Driving through the lush, montane forest at Ngorongoro was an unforgettable experience, as I waited to catch a sight of this, the largest crater in the world, 2,000 feet below us. As it happens, this is a far more exciting and scenic approach than it would be coming from the west, where the rim is much more open and bushy. Ngorongoro had only recently been declared a conservation area, and accommodation in the forest consisted of a few huts, which, retrospectively, added much to the sense of being in an animal paradise. I had already added many species to the notebook, from dull Streaky Seedeaters to more glamorous Broad-billed Rollers, and Jackson's Widowbirds bouncing up and down in the grass. (Considering that Sir Frederick Jackson discovered this bird, it is ironic, and sad, that the illustration in his book on the birds of Kenya and Uganda, one of my favourite works, actually shows the Long-tailed Widowbird. Can he have ever seen this painting of Lodge's? The book was published after his death.)

Next morning, the drive down the escarpment through the forest was slow and slippery, and a dank mist drifted eerily through the huge trees. Beautiful Golden-winged Sunbirds foraged in the dripping moss, and a leopard stared at us across a small gulley by the track, before lazily getting to its feet and disappearing. The floor of the crater was dotted with game, prides of indolent lions, and several rhinos with oxpeckers clambering around on them. Looking at this wealth of life, I could not help thinking how one of the largest volcanic explosions ever, only a few million years ago, had left a hole this size – about 100 square miles. How long did it take before it could become such a sanctuary?

A familiar looking bird by a small puddle near the car turned out to be a Green Sandpiper, and avocets and stints mingled with African specialities such as Kittliz's and Chestnut-banded Plovers. Lesser Flamingos and flocks of Avocets mingled with ducks, geese, spoonbills and herons in a lake, and a large flock of White Storks fed nearby, while more familiar Yellow Wagtails ran among them. Animals and birds were so abundant that one never knew where to look next, and the list of species in my notebook galloped ahead. Many of them had to be identified much later, when I had at last been able to buy a copy of Jackson's book.

A few days in this wildlife wilderness, and then it was time to head back to Uganda; the drive back from Nairobi to Nakuru was straight into the eye of the setting sun, and clouds of dust hardly improved things, but even so the planned stop for the night at Lake Nakuru turned out to be a real wash-out as far as birding went, the water level being so high we couldn't even get near the lake. The big yellow-barked acacias, which I was to walk happily around many times later, stood with their feet in the water.

Back in Kampala after another long drive, birding soon resumed, and indeed became almost frantic around Lake Victoria, and in the Botanical Gardens in Entebbe. A favoured locality was Port Bell, on the lake, where I watched Vieillot's Black Weavers busy round their nests, only for the proceedings to be rudely interrupted when my sister and I and a friend suddenly became aware that we were covered in ants, and had to strip off. Apart from that, I was listing and making notes about far more birds than I could identify at the time, and my only 'field guide' – a rather old edition of *Roberts' Birds of South Africa* – seemed more and more inadequate. I sometimes wonder whether in these days of fieldguides to everywhere,

birdwatchers make as many notes before turning to the book.

All too soon, my month had flown, but the notebooks remained, and confirmed my conviction that Uganda was a birdwatcher's delight, and that I must come back as soon as possible. For many reasons, my return was delayed far longer than I had hoped, though my next visit to East Africa allowed a far more extensive look at Kenya's birds, and I didn't get back to Uganda. The opportunity to make the acquaintance of many more African birds and countries came much later.

Northern Red Bishops.

13

Lake Baringo

One of the most breathtaking views anywhere in Africa opens up on your left as you drive northwards from Nairobi, along the edge of the highlands. There, far below in the shimmering heat, lies the Great Rift Valley, one of the grandest geological features on Earth. A gigantic volcanic fault, it runs from Mozambique in the south to the Jordan valley, where the Dead Sea is below sea level. The lakes of the Rift in East Africa vary amazingly in character – Natron is a soda waste, but Naivasha, which must sit on the highest elevation of the Rift at over 6,000 feet, is a blue resort of floating clumps of papyrus. A little further up the Rift is Nakuru, which I have seen both flooded and almost dry, and beyond that again, in lower country, are the brown waters of Baringo.

This area is a superb birding site, and the first time I came here I spent a week sketching the birds and their environment, but there is so much to see that a month would not have gone amiss. I grew particularly fond of watching a party of starlings that enlivened the cliffs, and apart from the fact that these were a local speciality around here, glossy starlings bring back poignant memories.

When I was about ten, we were visiting my grandmother in Bexhill. Amongst her friends was a Lady Jackson, and because I was interested in birds, we were invited to tea. She produced several stuffed glossy starlings for me to admire, from, of all places, a drawer in her bedroom! I was astounded, and had naturally never seen anything like them. Then she said that if I was still interested in birds by the time of my next visit, she would give me her copy of her late husband's book on the birds of Kenya and Uganda. I had no need to be told how generous this would be, and waited several weeks until we could go again. I was very disappointed to find that she had completely forgotten about this promise, but what was worse was that she had given the books to a church bazaar only a few days previously. (Many years later, I was shown beautiful skins of African birds kept in some else's dressing table drawers, but that is another story.)

The pale brown waters of the lake (*above*) looking towards the hills of the eastern flank of the Rift.

In the valley between the red cliffs of the Rift escarpment and Lake Baringo, Crested Francolins are always noisy, but there was a bird call in the low dry scrub nearby which is one of the characteristic sounds in acacia savanna in Kenya and northern Tanzania. It is a constantly and monotonously repeated 'chp chp chp' delivered quite slowly, and tracking down the author of this annoying sound became an early challenge at Baringo. As soon as it seemed the culprit had moved to a certain bush, the sound came from somewhere else nearby. I decided to sit down and wait. For sketching purposes, Barbara had constructed a lightweight stool, and I positioned myself on this, sketchbook in hand, in a suitable small clearing amongst the bushes.

Brown-tailed Rock Chat
Baringo, 11 oct 83

Baringo
11 oct 1983
Grey Wren Warbler

At last a movement close by disclosed a small grey bird, and as I raised my binoculars, the hessian on the stool gave way, and I fell heavily and noisily backwards into an extremely spiny bush. I was not going to give up getting a good look at this small warbler, and next day we went back and tape-recorded him very successfully. He sang, concealed, for six or seven minutes 'chup chup chup chp chp chup chp' on and on, and when we played the recording back he fell silent, and became a flitting shape circling around us in the bushes, finally flying just over our heads. Once, when very close to us, he could be seen to be keeping his bill half open – maybe panting in the heat – and once he called while performing an undulating song-flight over a bush – just a quick up and down. A dark grey little warbler with a red eye, and a longish tail which he cocked and waved, he reminded me of the Dartford Warblers which lurk in the spiny gorse on our English heathlands.

The parent Brown-tailed Rock Chat (*above*) perches attentively near its brood.

A few glimpses of the Grey Wren-Warbler (*left*) were all I could get as it skulked around in some impenetrable prickly bushes.

Very rangy, showing a lot of neck
and tail waving - will look rather
short beneath the forehead tufts.
Shy.

Bristle-crowned Starlings
Baringo   10 Oct 83

Parties of Bristle-crowned Starlings (*above*) were a feature of the cliffs, but seemed rather shy, and stayed quite high up. They were very active and sociable, whistling away as they moved among the rocks and bushes on the cliff-face with their long tails waving about.

The red cliffs at Baringo
11 Oct 1993

The red cliffs near Lake Baringo (*above*) are part of the western ramparts of the Rift Valley, and they are home to the Bristle-crowned Starling, the most rakish of all the glossy starlings, many of which, though beautifully iridescent – "shining like polished metal" someone has said – are rather dumpy birds. These cliff-dwellers have a curious tuft of bristles on the forehead which gives them a rather flat-headed look, and also gives them their vernacular name. They also have one of the longest tails of all the starlings, and seemingly the most flexible. They are birds of low-lying dry country in north-east Africa, where there are cliffs or rocky outcrops and gorges, and though sociable, and often quite noisy, are shy and difficult to get close to.

These drawings were made with the aid of a telescope as the birds flew around the cliffs, perching on rocks and trees, the long wavy tails of individuals sometimes crossing as if they were fencing.

I am always tempted to sketch the habitat of birds that frequent spectacular scenery like these cliffs, though far too often the opportunity or time does not allow it. Birding on the move, and trying to see many different species as possible, is simply not compatible with anything other than rapid notes or what, for some reason, are called 'thumbnail sketches'. However, sitting down quietly – even to make a drawing of an aesthetically pleasing termite mound – often allows wildlife to appear of its own accord. Making a watercolour of the Baringo cliffs took enough time for me to get a feel for what goes on up there; a Hemprich's Hornbill suddenly appeared and sailed along the cliffs, flapping and gliding. It was the male, who a little while ago arrived to take food to the female in a nest hole in a rather bulbous protuberance in the rock-face. The starlings were very active, and then something much grander excited them, as a pair of Verreaux's Eagles floated along the cliff face. One bird dropped down to the nest, unnoticed before, a huge heap of sticks about six feet tall, in a vertical fissure, with some boulders underneath. The large chick – maybe a couple of months old – stood up to greet its parent. It was mainly white, with some dark blotching, and would grow into one of the handsomest of all eagles.

A mile or two north of the lodge at Baringo, there is a flat stretch of ground, with scattered acacias and tangled, creeping vines, where there is ample evidence of the volcanic origins of the country, the whole place being strewn with rocks and lumps of lava. The tall, conical termite mounds could be taken for mock-ups of the volcanoes which spewed fire and brimstone at early man around here, and one almost expects to see little spirals of smoke coming from them. We had found a pair of Spotted Thicknees here – a larger version of our Stone-curlew – and went back one evening to look at them. By going slowly, we could approach to within about twenty yards, while they stood in the shade of a small bush.

I suddenly became aware of a smaller bird standing stock-still much closer, and then another close to it. A pair of Heuglin's Coursers had relied on their cryptic plumage and immobility to avoid being noticed, and had nearly succeeded, and then – even better – we saw they had a well-grown chick

with them. As we kept very quiet and still, they relaxed a bit, and moved away a little – not very far – and it was some fifteen minutes before they disappeared. When on the alert, they stretched the neck up, and the big eye was wide open, but when they relaxed the head sank on the shoulders, and the eye half closed. For ten minutes or so we just looked at them, while I memorised the stance and markings. Then I was able to make some rough sketches and notes in the little sketchbook which I always carried, and worked them up back at camp. This system works well on a birding walk as opposed to a sketching trip – but is even better when one can re-locate a bird and check out the first impressions. That is also essential when making a page of studies of a bird moving around and showing different aspects of its plumage.

The Heuglin's Coursers (*below*) with their single chick.

Heuglin's Courser
Baringo 14 october 1983

when alarmed the neck is stretched stiffly out and up, but when relaxed the head sinks into the shoulder and the eyes are ½ shut

long yellow legs, and back very evenly patterned with dark centres to the feathers

back view

The baby crouched motionless while we watched – the cheek patch is pale yellow buff – rufous in adults.

Termite mound, basalt rocks
and shrubs
Baringo 13 oct 83

A study of a termite mound (*above*) amongst scrubby vegetation, with bushes and vines near the lake. The ground is littered with lumps of lava, a reminder of the region's explosive past.

The adult Heuglin's Courser (*right*).

walking slowly away among the lava rubble

19

Baringo 11 oct 1983
Slate coloured Boubou.

When calling, the bill is pointed
down and the neck arched, and
the bird bobs slightly at each call.

Studies of the Slate-coloured Boubou.

Baringo
13 oct 1983
Mouse-coloured Penduline Tit

Amongst the many bird calls in the scrub around Baringo are the varied fluty duets of a real skulker, the Slate-coloured Boubou (*far left*) which necessitated careful stalking, and I found that the best way to get good views was to call it up with a tape recorder, which worked quite well. These studies were made as it moved closer in the bushes, responding to the recording of its own calls. This is a bush-shrike with habits quite unlike the open-country shrikes of Europe that perch on prominent look-outs. I made a few drawings of it, and noticed that when it calls, the neck is arched and the bill pointed down, while the bird bobs slightly. The bush-shrikes are a family of noisy but shy birds, usually going around in pairs and difficult to see in the thick cover they frequent; the boubous are mostly black or black and white, while the gonoleks sport brilliant crimson – or yellow – underparts. All are famous for their duetting, which advertises a pair's territory in dense vegetation. One bird makes two or three melodious, resonant notes, immediately answered by the other bird, often with harsh or scolding sounds, though the calls are very variable, and both birds often call at the same time, or overlap.

The dull-sounding **Mouse-coloured Penduline Tit (*left*)** is a tiny little bird that forages amongst the spiny branches of the acacia trees, and only occurs in a few dry areas of North-east Africa. I was sure this bird had a nest nearby, but failed to find it. These African penduline tits build beautiful little nests, like a little bag, with a side entrance, suspended from a twig.

21

Hemprich's Hornbill
Baringo 11 oct 83.

Lakeside birding offered some colourful sketching opportunities in the form of the red and yellow bishops, members of the weaver family. They buzzed about, looking like big, fiery bumble-bees, swaying and fluttering in the reeds, their plumage all fluffed up. The Northern Red Bishop is the species here, at practically the southernmost limit of its range in Africa, which extends north through the Sudan and west to Mauritania. One difference from other red bishop species lies in the fact that the long upper-tail coverts conceal the tail. The other bishop here, the little Yellow-crowned Bishop, is, by contrast, one of the most widely distributed birds of its family in Africa.

The **Hemprich's Hornbills (*above*)** were constantly flying to and fro along the cliff face in their slow, buoyant way. Like the Bristle-crowned Starlings, they only occur in North-east Africa, and need cliffs or rock faces where they nest in inaccessible crevices.

Northern Red and Yellow-crowned Bishops (*right*).

Lake Baringo - 12 Oct 1983

Red and Yellow-crowned Bishops
Note that in this species of Red Bishop —
Euplectes franciscanus - the upper tail coverts
are very long and practically conceal
the tail.

23

Nothing could be more of a contrast with the busy sociable weavers than a solitary woodpecker which obligingly posed for a quick drawing. Woodpeckers are often difficult to see, and always seem to want to search the far side of a trunk or branch. Consequently, I made extremely few drawings of them, though there are nearly 30 species in Africa. This **Nubian Woodpecker (*right*)** is one of the commonest and most easily seen in East Africa.

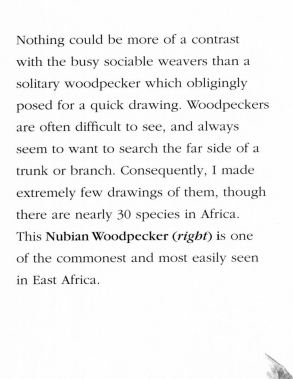

Nubian
Woodpecker

Crown and nape red. A dull red moustachial stripe. Sides of face greyish white with even fine streaking - a white line over ear coverts is wider over the eye. Heavy concentric blotching on breast becomes sparser below. Thin shaft lines of coverts widen on wing tip to blobs near barb in overall finely barred shafts of tail feathers brighter golden. Ventral aspect of tail pale yellowy white

Lake Baringo
9 Ocr 83

Lake Baringo
9 Ocr 83
White-bellied Go-away Bird

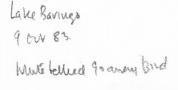

The noisy **White-bellied Go-away Bird (*left*)** – so-called from its nasal 'swearing' – is a savanna turaco, quite lacking the beautiful plumage of its woodland cousins, but its bold simple patterning, perky crest, and size makes it a striking bird of the open savanna not easily missed.

Lake Baringo
12 oct. 1983
Vitelline Masked Weavers

Vitelline Masked Weavers were nesting in acacias near the lake. There is so much going on at a weaver colony – even a small one like this – that it is difficult to know what to start drawing. I needed to make notes for distinguishing it from similar weavers (red eyes, small bill, small black throat patch) but I found it a challenge to capture the various poses as the birds swung and fluttered around their new nests.

Black-billed Turacos — in dappled palm
in Kakamega 19 oct 83

26

A western Kenyan forest

It has always surprised me how people can look so neat and tidy when living in the sort of place where rain turns the roads into mud baths. I was reminded of this when driving to the Kakamega forest reserve along an extremely bumpy and muddy road. There were people streaming along in both directions, dressed immaculately in their Sunday best, whereas I, in a vehicle, felt hot and distinctly unkempt. Eight miles of this road led to the forestry rest-house – a substantial wooded structure on massive stilts. Here we settled in to our room, at the end of a lovely balcony that overlooked the edge of the forest, only forty feet away. In the first hour, before we even went for a walk, we saw a number of new birds from this balcony, including the beautiful Lühder's Bush-shrike, but had given little thought to more mundane matters. When we came to cook an evening meal, we kindled a fire in the kitchen, and found we had to borrow a (very old) saucepan and two spoons, and immediately afterwards a hurricane lamp, by the light of which we ate baked beans. Our hand torch had run out of battery, and the borrowed lamp gave out only just enough light to write notes by.

The manager who kindly provided these items called himself the 'guest-in-charge', and was one Leonard, who certainly knew his birds and was able to point them out to us. He was very friendly, showing us round, helping with the bags and so on. One morning we had to go in to Kakamega,

braving the appalling road, and foolishly, as it turned out, asked Leonard if he wanted anything, in view of the loan of the saucepan. A blanket would be very nice, he said. It was not inexpensive.

We were the only guests, and he was the only other person with a key to our room, despite which we wondered for some days as to why our small supply of cash seemed to be dwindling. We eventually came to the conclusion that he must have been helping himself, apparently taking some each day, so that we were puzzled but not suspicious. Not content with that, he bombarded us with letters for months afterwards wanting money for his daughter's school fees. He was very good on his birds, though.

Kakemega is the easternmost outlier of the great central belt of African rainforest, so it is the only area in Kenya where one can see some of the true forest birds which occur commonly further west; it also has an interesting flora, with some 130 tree species. When we visited this precious relic of ancient forest, it covered 22,000 acres, yet it is in one of Kenya's most densely populated regions and, despite its reserve status, Kakemega has been constantly encroached upon, especially for tea cultivation. Near the Rest House, the forest is bisected with a convenient grid system of paths, constructed by the ornithologist Dale Zimmerman for research work in the 1960s. His clearings and paths make for easy birding.

A sun-dappled path in the forest at Kakamega, and above it, a pair of Black-billed Turacos flash their crimson wings before disappearing in the canopy (*left*).

Blue shouldered Robin Chat
Kakamega 21 Oct 83

One of my early target birds in the forest at Kakamega was the **Blue-shouldered Robin-Chat (*above*)**, a retiring thrush, relative of the much more easily seen White-browed Robin-Chat. All the members of this family are renowned songsters. A particular feature of this species' repertoire is its superb mimicking – I had read about this ability, but the fact was brought home straight away. Leonard had heard a whistle, and we knelt down in the wet mud on the path to try and get a glimpse of the bird through the sun-dappled undergrowth. I was not sure which particular call he had drawn attention to, when, from quite close by I heard the unmistakable first seven notes of The Archers' signature tune in a beautiful plangent whistle, taken slowly and with a slight rubato, which made it very funny and instantly memorable. Knowing the jingle only

too well, I whistled back 'Too ti-too ti-too ti-too'. It responded quite enthusiastically, keeping well hidden, while we crouched ever lower in the mud, trying to catch a glimpse of it. At last it moved to a branch just above the ground, where the head and forepart of the body were in a little shaft of sunlight, which glinted on the cerulean patch on its shoulder. Subsequently, we had several views of it on the forest floor, moving about in the patchy sunlight about twenty feet away. It was very smart, with the black mask enhanced by the white supercilium, and contrasting with the russet breast. Several years later, we netted seven Blue-shouldered Robin-Chats in the forest at Minziro, in north-west Tanzania, and I was able to study them in the cage at my leisure. (Incidentally, these constituted the first record of the species from Tanzania.)

Amongst the more 'difficult' forest birds to identify are the greenbuls, and I had made a key to the significant features and calls, but the first one I drew was an unidentified species (*below*) hopping up a vine stem. Every time I made a quick sketch, and then looked up, it was a little higher, and facing the

opposite direction, or looking up and not down, so I had the impression of a series of images, a sort of kaleidoscope effect, of many birds along the same vine stem. It was such an attractive combination of action and postures that, though I hesitate to say it, identification seemed not to matter much!

I know that this will sound scandalous to some birdwatchers, but the fact is that warblers are often dull. They don't have much in the way of structure to be interesting subjects to draw and, for the most part, you have to go to America to find warblers that are colourful – many of the Old World ones are endless shades of brown or olive. They skulk. The great American bird artist Louis Agassiz Fuertes even remarked that 'the difference between warblers and no warblers is very slight', and here was a man who knew such birds as the Golden-winged Warbler! However, the Black-faced Rufous Warbler, (*overleaf*) at Kakamega and all points west, is an exception, being boldly marked, conspicuous, and active in the forest undergrowth. I could hardly overlook two that were churring at something in a small clearing by a fallen log, and I had good close views as they moved about. The simple colour combination of rufous and black is appealing on a small bird.

Kakamega
18 ocv 83

Progress of a greenbul
up a vine stem

Equatorial Akalat
Kakamega Forest
20 ocv 1983

Kakamega's version of the European Robin, the **Equatorial Akalat** (*right*) is a bird endemic to eastern Africa, though it has seven close relatives, all having quite restricted distributions across the forest parts of central Africa. Although often difficult to see, this individual sat close by the path on a little twig, as if interested to see us.

Studies of Black-faced Rufous Warblers.

Black-faced Rufous Warbler
Kahamaa 19 oct 83

One of the most attractive of all the small birds is the delicate African Blue Flycatcher (*below*). It is a bird of central and western African forests, and just reaches into Kenya at Kakamega. It was sometimes called the Blue Fairy Flycatcher, which is a prettier name, and somehow evokes its character. Like a pale blue elfin light flickering in the gloom of the forest, it is an active and quite a noisy little sprite. It pirouettes around tree trunks and logs, twisting from side to side, fanning and flirting the tail and drooping the wings. It is charming. Many flycatchers are rather solitary, and only draw attention to themselves when they suddenly launch into the air after an insect, but this fairy is too vivacious to be solitary.

The Blue Flycatcher flirts its tail.

Blue Flycatcher
Kakamega Forest
18 Oct 83.

Light and shade at the edge of
a clearing - Kakamega Forest
18 Oct '83

Light and shade at the edge of a clearing
at Kakamega - a pencil study done at a
time when the birding had gone quiet.

A bird flew up into tall open trees, and as he landed he cocked the tail up - back to us - showing the white belly and thighs and the long yellow-based, black tipped tail. Plumage a bright turquoise - in oily petrol colour. Shortly afterwards, another bird came sailing in to land on a thick branch. Tail up, wings drooped and crest raised.

Great Blue Turacos
Kakamega Forest
20 Oct '83

A large and unmistakable bird of central and western African forests is the **Great Blue Turaco** (*above*), the largest and grandest member of a family peculiar to Africa, whose range just extends into Kenya at Kakamega. One bird flew up into a tall tree in a clearing, cocking its tail right up as it landed, showing the rufous belly and thighs, and the long yellow and blue, black-tipped tail. Shortly afterwards, another bird came sailing in to land on a big branch, tail and crest up and wings drooped. These birds have quite a long neck, and are quite agile and bouncy, despite weighing about as much as a Mallard.

33

Red-headed Malimbe
Kakamega Forest
20 OCV 83

Searches branches rather like a
Nuthatch, hanging upside down
or creeping upwards peering
into crevices — more like a
tit, really. The bird is actually
jet black

Studies of Red-headed Malimbes.

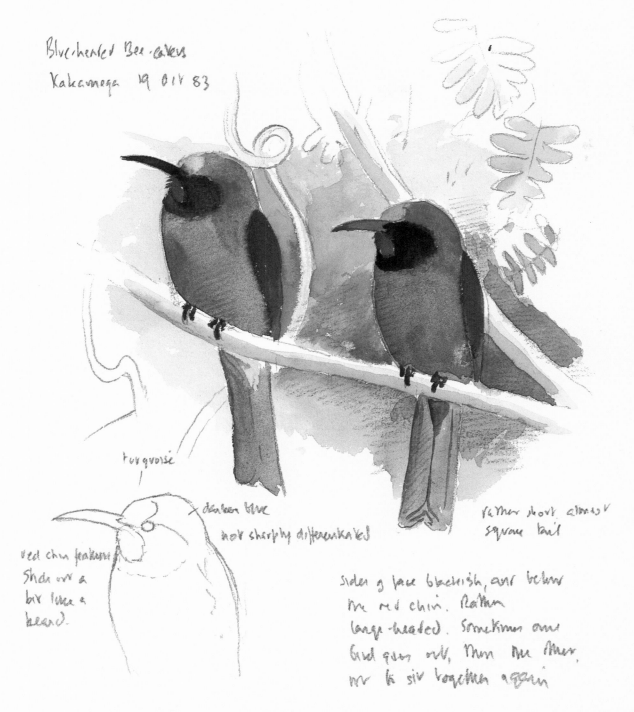

Blue-headed Bee-eaters
Kakamega 19 OCT 83

turquoise

darker blue
not sharply differentiated

rather short almost
square tail

red chin feathers
Sticks out a
bit like a
beard.

sides of face blackish, and below
the red chin. Rather
large-headed. Sometimes one
bird goes out, then the other,
nor to sit together again

We watched a pair of Red-headed Malimbes – a sort of arboreal weaver – for minutes as they foraged around the branches of a very tall tree over a stream. They moved just like nuthatches, hanging upside-down, peering into crevices and creeping around the boughs. Quite a small but well-defined group amongst the weavers, the malimbes all sport a colour combination of red and black, and the females are very similar in appearance to their mates.

The Blue-headed Bee-eater is one of three African species which are basically forest birds, the others being the Black and the Black-headed Bee-eater. The first two, in particular, look quite different from their open-country cousins, which are mostly shades of greens, yellows and chestnut – the Carmine Bee-eater being an exception. The forest birds are much darker shades of black, blue and chestnut, and also differ in being sedentary – many of the others are strongly migratory. Not surprisingly, they are mostly birds of western and central Africa, and the Blue-headed is the only one that gets into Kenya, and that only in the Kakamega forest. It is quite a confiding little bird, and on many days we watched a pair who would sit together at the edge of a little clearing, about 30 feet up. Now and then, one or the other would swoop out after a fly, sometimes returning to the same perch, sometimes not.

Blue-headed Bee-eaters (*above*).

Around Naivasha and Nairobi

After you turn off the main road to drive round Naivasha, there is a small bridge over a lush little stream. We were on our way to stay at Korongo Farm, on the lake-shore, and stopped by the bridge, but only very briefly, since the first thing we saw was a puff-adder, coiled fatly by the parapet. It moved, I thought, somewhat reluctantly when it saw us, and slid noiselessly into the vegetation. That was the end of our stream-side walk.

A bath was the first necessity after our drive from Kakamega, but then there was time for a walk through open, grazed areas along the marshy lake-shore, with its great rafts of papyrus. The trees around the lake are the big, yellow-barked acacias, just as at Lake Nakuru, and aware of how often one can find owls in these trees, I wasn't too surprised when Barbara spotted the big daddy of them all – Verreaux's Eagle Owl – looking at us over his shoulder. The hooded eyes, with their pink eyelids, always remind me of a certain film star, but I am never quite sure which one – it may be Garbo, or Bette Davis. I liked the combination of this huge owl, almost dwarfed among the stout branches of these waterside acacias, and made a couple of drawings, one of which – setting the owl in a more detailed background of branches and twigs – I later used as the basis for an oil painting (see page 44).

The big, laconic Verreaux's Eagle Owl (*right*) with its characteristic film-star eyelids.

Great White Pelicans at Naivasha (*below*).

One of a number of studies I made of a captive Crowned Eagle (*left*), a rather fearsome bird, about which there is more to say on page 53.

Study of a papyrus clump evidently
done at a quiet time for birds!

38

Papyrus clump
Naivasha   28 oct 83

Another drawing of the owl to get
more background material for a
possible painting.

Verreaux's Eagle Owl
Naivasha
26 oct 83

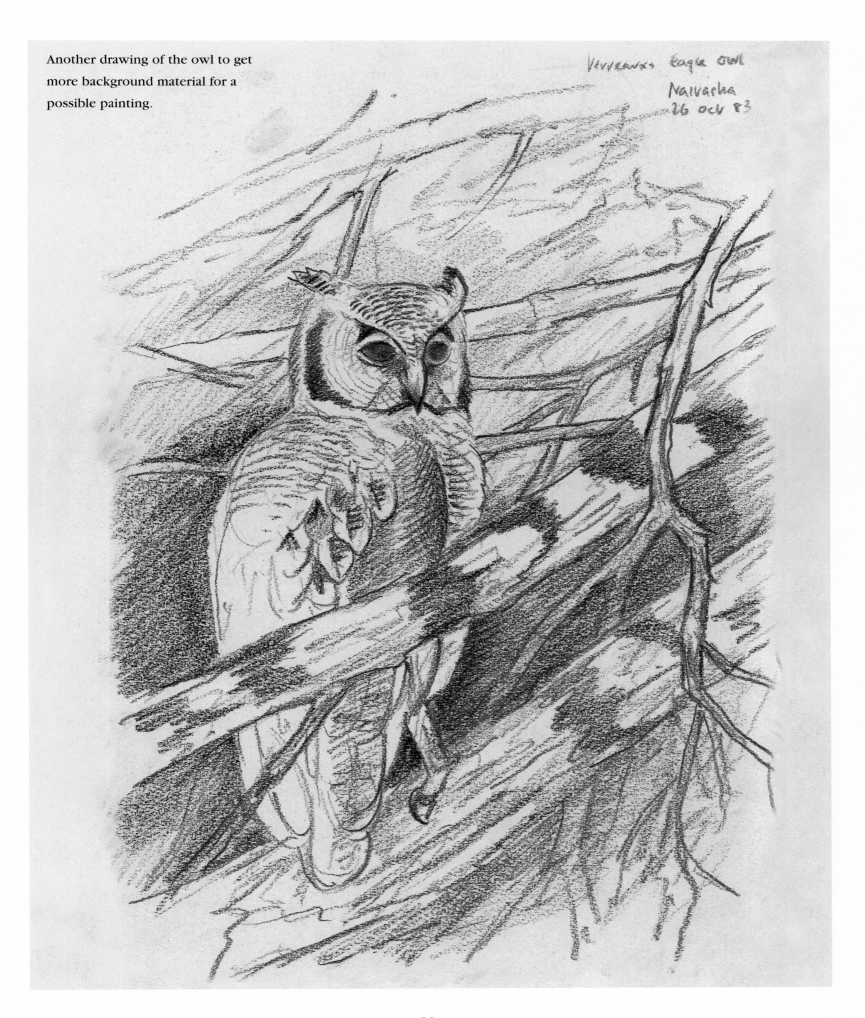

Green-backed Heron Naivasha

Pelicans in the papyrus
Naivasha 28 Oct 83

40

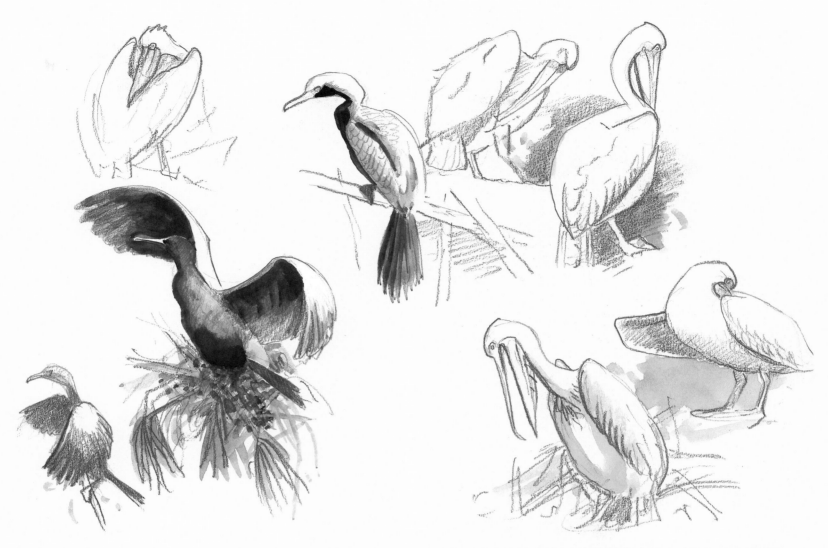

Always a solitary waterside bird, the Striated Heron (*above, left*) was drawn at the Crater Lake.

The waterbirds provided plenty of sketching material, and I even sat down, braving the mozzies, to make a pencil study of a papyrus clump, and then, feeling this had been rather an academic exercise, made another drawing of **papyrus with a group of pelicans and a Long-tailed Cormorant (*lower, left*)**. Watching the **pelicans and cormorants moving about and preening (*above*)** could easily have occupied a whole day, and that without paying any attention to the herons and egrets of half a dozen species, Pied and Malachite Kingfishers, noisy Hadada Ibises and Egyptian Geese, while birds such as the Scaly-throated Honeyguide only merited a mention in the notebook.

Pelicans (*right*) on the ground – or water – look such massive, heavy birds that it is always a surprise at how aerial they are, how buoyant, and how adept at soaring in thermals. Small parties would always be floating in over the lake, hardly flapping, coasting silently down like a squadron of planes that had cut their engines.

Several days were spent on the farm, drawing and painting, without having to go anywhere else to find subjects. Birds that I was able to study at leisure included the **African Green Pigeons**, (*above*) which can be a difficult subject, as they are rather inclined to move quietly and slowly around in thick foliage. One can be under a tree with pigeons in it without being at all aware of their presence, and it is always a surprise to see how many fly out when they are flushed.

Crater lake
nr Kenngo
Naivasha

We met three nice Americans at the farm, and spent a long time discussing birds, people, Kenya and so forth, and on the following day one of them – a Dr Gordon Brown – drove us out to a local haunt known as Crater Lake (*above*) on the land of an adjoining farm. It is indeed a crater, about a mile across, with quite steep sides clothed in dense undergrowth. One shrub was rather like vervain, but much bigger, with very prickly seedpods which attached themselves abundantly to us. The big acacias formed quite a close canopy overhead. The lake at the bottom had evidently expanded relatively recently, as many dead tree trunks and branches made a tangle in the water around the edge. A Striated Heron fished here, and I was able to work up a tolerably finished pencil drawing while it moved slowly around. The lake also supported many fish-eagles and Little Grebes. A new warbler with a very loud trilling song hunted around in the undergrowth – the **Grey-capped Warbler** (*left*).

Sunbirds were common in the gardens at Korongo, particularly Variable and Scarlet-chested, a pair of which had made a nest in a bush just outside our chalet (*left*), not a particularly tidy structure, but a good subject for a drawing in the heat of the day. The female would often sit with her head just showing, listening to the male chirruping away nearby. This is probably the commonest open-country sunbird in the whole of Africa, but an almost identical species – Hunter's Sunbird – occurs only in the dry lowlands of north-east Africa.

The **Tawny-flanked Prinia** (*right*) is even more widely distributed in Africa than the sunbird, and is the sort of commonplace bird that rarely gets a second look. This one near Hell's Gate was fossicking about in the grass, flirting its tail and calling its dry little note continuously; it found its way into the sketchbook in the absence of anything more noteworthy.

The **Verreaux's Eagle Owl** (*left*) sketch eventually became the basis for this somewhat impressionist oil painting, in which I tried to convey how the huge owl is dwarfed by massive branches of the yellow-barked acacia.

45

Hells gate
Naivasha
25 oct 83

An excursion to Hell's Gate (*above*) made a complete contrast to the rather claustrophobic feel of the crater lake. This scenic geological feature is a great rent in the hills around Naivasha, formed when the lake was once far higher, and, probably as a result of some cataclysmic volcanic event or earthquake, gushed out of its basin. The wide grassy plain only serves to emphasise the towering cliff – 400 or 500 feet high – where there were many swifts and Rüppell's Griffon Vultures, though we did not see the Lammergeiers which are usually here. There are two isolated towers of rock, and various other cliffs, roughly forming two sides of a long valley. A herd of zebra and kongoni grazed quietly near the track, with some giraffes and Thomson's gazelles. A gawky Secretary Bird flew over with its great long legs sticking out, and the tail a bit longer still. We watched it stamping on a small snake in the grass in a manic dance, like someone who has inadvertently trodden on a column of fire-ants, jumping about, half opening its wings to balance, all legs and tail and action.

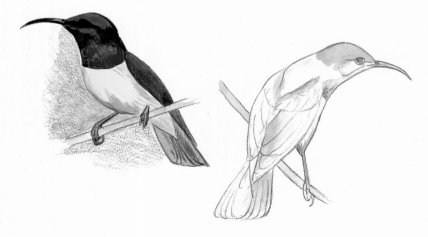

The Variable Sunbird (*left*) is one of the commonest and most widely distributed of all the sunbirds in Africa.

Over a period of years, I made many visits to the country around Nairobi, often staying with friends in whose gardens I could sit and draw birds at leisure. Billy and Nancy Cooper were among the earliest of friends whose generosity and hospitality made a world of difference. On one occasion they made their Toyota Landcruiser available to us for six weeks. We returned about ten days later than planned, and they were so relieved that we were still alive, and the vehicle in one piece, that they threw a memorable party. The following morning we witnessed an avian drama, watching an African Hawk Eagle trying, and failing, to catch Green Pigeons, but trying to draw a rapid sequence of events with a shaky hand and a throbbing head was an experience too far. I made a

much better version the next day, which somehow brought to mind Wordsworth's definition of poetry, as 'the recollection of emotion in tranquillity'. The Toyota, which was an old model, was christened 'The Monstrosity', and lumbered along at a very regal pace, consuming fuel as if it was a Formula 1 Ferrari. At its best, we covered nearly ten miles to the gallon, but it could be made to go almost anywhere.

Some warbler drawings (*below*) made at Korongo farm; the dumpy little Red-faced Crombec and the more elegant Yellow-breasted Apalis are both characteristic birds of acacia woodlands in this area.

26 ocv 83
Korongo farm,
Naivasha

Although quite agile it is not especially vivacious in its movements like a tit - almost deliberate at times.

Yellow-breasted Apalis

Crombec. Foraging and singing in acacia. Often hangs upside down and extends neck or twists head while searching for insects. Has a short rather scratchy song repeated several times - rather quiet.

Black Kite.
Karen.   7 Nov 1990

The **Black Kite studies (*left and above*)** were made while sitting at a table in Billy Cooper's garden in the shade, no doubt with refreshment at hand. In fact, one of the delights of Nairobi is that it is a city with a wonderful birdlife, so there is no shortage of subjects, and in gardens they can be studied at leisure and in comfort.

Naro Moru, 7 Nov.

Dusky Flycatcher –
very tame, iv often sav
within a few feet and
took no notice of me.

Two garden birds which are easy to see are the **Olive Thrush (*right*)** and the **Dusky Flycatcher (*above*)**. The latter is a delightful little bird, often extremely tame – or at any rate unconcerned at humans close by – even a few feet away. I have a particular affection for flycatchers, and it is sad that the Spotted Flycatcher is becoming increasingly rare in English gardens. The regularity of its habits, sitting quietly on watch, then making an adroit sally for an insect and returning to its perch, make it as familiar and predictable a part of the garden scene as a flowerbed. A pair, possibly the same individuals, were welcome summer tenants of our Kentish garden, as if pleased to take up lodging with us again, and I always enjoyed finding the nest in a creeper on the house. In bad weather, they took to sitting on the croquet hoops, no doubt unaware that on fine days, during summer visits of the three (competitive) editors of *The Birds of Africa*, these same hoops saw and heard a lot more action.

Olive Thrush, Karen

A very different looking bird, but a proper flycatcher, is the **White-eyed Slaty Flycatcher** (*left*) also a bird of gardens in Kenya, in that these resemble the forest-edge habitat which is its real home. However, it is much more of a gleaner than the Spotted Flycatcher, taking insects off the ground or a branch as much as by pursuing them in the air.

Despite many visits to the Nairobi National Park, I have never been able to do much drawing there, so the sketch of the **Long-tailed Fiscal – the largest of the fiscal shrikes – is a one-off** (*right*). Part of its attraction as a subject was the whistling thorn, with its black ant-galls built around the spines. I made a more detailed study of this plant at Naro Moru (on page 65) with a view to using it in a painting of some appropriate bird, but have not yet done so.

Simon Thompsett's eagles
Nairobi

Crowned Eagle threat display

Martial Eagle.

On one occasion, I was taken to see a collection of birds of prey, kept by Simon Thompsett at his place near the Athi river. These were birds which had either been injured, or had fallen out of nests or otherwise needed care and attention. They included a Martial Eagle and a fearsome Crowned Eagle, and this was a prime opportunity to study and sketch, in detail, birds one could never hope to get close to in the wild.

Leslie Brown made lengthy life studies of the Crowned Eagle, and had one pair under continuous observation for twenty years. He describes finding a half-grown bushbuck on which one of the eagles had dropped, and then overpowered, as the animal flailed about on the ground, despite it being twice the eagle's own weight. Monkeys are a regular prey, being knocked off a branch with a heavy downward blow, and killed on the ground. The famous bird painter David Reid-Henry kept one of these magnificent eagles at his home in north London, and he

would carry it on the underground on his wrist. No health and safety problems then.

Simon's bird was certainly spirited and aggressive, and he told me that it had taken prey as large as small gazelles, not to mention somebody's dog. I drew it while it sat on his wrist, but I don't think it liked me, and put on a scary threat display, thrusting its head forward with the crown feathers raised, puffing out the neck hackles and drooping its wings. The feet of this eagle are exceptionally heavy and powerful, and I can imagine the force of the grip which would drive the long talons deep into prey. I once handled a tiny owl in Malaysia, about the size of a Corn Bunting, and the grip of its feet – quite large for the size of the bird – around my gloved thumb was astonishing. The Crowned Eagle is well adapted to its need for agility in a forest environment, with its short, very broad wings, and the long, ample tail, enabling it to manoeuvre like a giant sparrowhawk.

53

Crowned Eagle
— c threat display
Athi river Upper 88

The aggression of the **Crowned Eagle** (*above*) was alarming, especially at close quarters. That apart, it is an extremely handsome and impressive raptor, whose beautiful plumage markings and size can best be appreciated in captivity.

The **Martial Eagle** (*right, and overleaf*) was a much more docile individual, and took no exception to me. It is said to be much more difficult to study in the wild than the Crowned Eagle, being noticeably shyer. It spends much time soaring at great heights, and is the largest African eagle, very much an open country and savanna bird, preying on game birds and mammals up to the size of impala calves. It is a very heavy and powerful predator, though the feet are in fact not quite as massive as the awe-inspiring talons of its shorter-winged and longer-tailed cousin.

Martial Eagle

Athi river, Kenya

Sept 88

Marhal Eagle.
Athi River. Kenya
Sept 1988

The **Fischer's Starlings (*above*)** were drawn while we stayed for a few days at Kulalu ranch, near Tsavo East, where Rod and Shirley Paterson run 10,500 head of cattle on 250,000 acres. They have built a house on a rise overlooking the Galana river about a mile away, and created a garden around it in only five years. Being a pretty dry area, the local birds appreciate the pawpaw put out daily on the bird-table, and Wattled and Fischer's Starlings are common visitors; cattle troughs out on the ranch are inclined to leak, and are consequently also a great attraction for birds. The cattle, incidentally, have admirers of their own. This is not far from the area where the 'man-eaters of Tsavo', made famous in Col. Patterson's book of that name, terrorised the coolies building the Mombasa to Nairobi railway in the early years of the 20th century. The descendants of those lions had, the week before we visited the Patersons, taken 25 head of cattle, and on one night alone a pride of ten lions came in and killed and ate 18 cows!

One morning we went out for an early walk through the riverside scrub with David Pearson and Miles Coverdale, and learnt of the necessity to talk sufficiently loudly so that any lurking buffalos were not taken by surprise. I had previously thought that if I came suddenly on a buffalo, it would have been me who would be the surprised party, but I took the advice. Some years later, on foot in quite thick bush in the Serengeti, we were confident about where the buffalos were because of the direction the oxpeckers were flying, until they started returning in our direction, and we beat a prudent retreat.

Birdlife around the ranch and along the Galana river was abundant, and included migrants from eastern Europe such as Thrush Nightingales and an Upcher's Warbler, and local specialities such as the beautiful Golden Pipit and the Pangani Longclaw, both birds characteristic of the dry east African grasslands. Less immediately attractive, and less flighty, were the flocks of Chestnut-headed Sparrow-Larks, and the commoner White-browed Sparrow-Weavers which hopped around the leaky cattle troughs, and I was able to draw these and a good variety of other birds, including the lovely Rosy-patched Shrike, with splashes of red along the throat and on the rump.

Chestnut-headed Sparrow-Larks (*top*),
Black-headed Weavers (*right*) and a
Yellow-fronted Canary (*above*).

Black-headed Weaver
Tsavo   22 Nov 83

White-browed Sparrow-Weavers (*left*) are a common and widespread species in eastern and southern Africa.

3 Nov 83
Whitebrowed Sparrow-Weaver

Tsavo. 23 november.
Rosy-patched Shrike –
very long and rangey with
long tail & neck
Scarlet rump

The Rosy-patched Shrike (*right*) is a lovely slender shrike of open country, endemic to North-east Africa. One singing from the top of a bush at dawn, with the sun glinting on his breast, was a fine sight, and I have seen several males duetting close together.

We had been originally introduced to the Coverdales by David Pearson – or rather he had given us their names as people at the coast who might be able to show us the local birds. When we turned up at their lovely house on the beach at Diani, we were slightly disconcerted to find they were not there. We put up our small tent on the beach, and had a hot night, wondering what to do should they not return. Fortunately, they returned the next day, and we were able to enjoy their splendid hospitality for the first time, and since then we have had many enjoyable safaris with them.

Ringing waders at Mida Creek with Miles and Liz was a memorable experience. We set the nets up a few hundred yards from the shore, paddling out in warm water not much above our ankles, with the soft mud squidging up between our toes. The birds fly in to the nets in the dark, and the most charismatic prize, when we came to see what we had caught, were the beautiful and enigmatic Crab Plovers. While they were being measured and ringed, they lay on their backs in our laps, quite unfazed, and watched us with their beautiful great luminous eyes. They didn't flap, scratch, bite or struggle, and indeed behaved impeccably. They were stunning. There was no opportunity to draw on this occasion, and indeed, while we were able to see many new birds of the coastal forests, I did not succeed in getting much down on paper.

It was very dry when we were in the wonderful forest reserve at Sokoke, just inland from Mida creek, which has a number of very interesting birds, and a surprising and sudden change in soil colour from white to red in places. Birding was difficult – drawing even more so. The Retz's Helmet-Shrikes in Sokoke (*below*) were an exception, but much to my disappointment we failed to see the local speciality, the tiny Sokoke Scops Owl, as we were on our own, and did not know where to look. As ever, the problem with forest birds is that they are elusive and difficult to see well, and the best way to get any worthwhile drawing done is to concentrate on whatever is showing best, and memorize as much as possible. On this occasion, we did not have nets. The helmet-shrikes, which get their name from the bristly crest on the forehead, were very active, moving restlessly through the trees in fairly open foliage, quite frequently hovering or fluttering to pick insects off leaves. When perched, they often crane the neck and peer about in all directions as they search the foliage. Unlike most shrikes, they are conspicuously social and noisy birds.

Sokoke Forest
26 Nov
Retz's Redbilled Shrike

Hovering to flick insect off leaf

Retz's Red-billed Shrikes.

60

Singing Cisticolas
Crown deep rich sqv chestnut brown, unstreaked
mantle greyish brown, greater wents and flight
feathers upper edged Tail blackish-brown
Eye madder, legs pale dull pinkish-brown
Mouth black' - A bartes in tangled rank undergrowth.

Singing Cisticolas.

The Aberdare National Park was established in 1950, and is a wonderful area of montane moorland and forest in the central highlands of Kenya, where there is one of the best-known game lodges in all Africa – Treetops. Not aspiring to such luxury, we paid a visit over one New Year to the Aberdares with Billy and Nancy Cooper, staying in modest but perfectly accceptable accommodation at Fisherman's Camp. The trout fishing in the Aberdares, in the icy clear streams, is said to be excellent, and there is an abundance of wildlife from rhinos and elephants to the rarely-seen forest antelope, the bongo. Birding is given an extra dimension in these beautiful surroundings, and we could have done with very much longer there. While admiring one of the many waterfalls, we became aware of some Slender-billed Starlings, living in a totally different environment from the lanky Fischer's Starlings of the dry low-country bush.

Two of these slender, glossy birds were nesting in a small dark recess surrounded by vegetation near the top of a waterfall. They were quite wary, but now and again one would sit on a bush nearby long enough for me to get some details down, and the initial drawing rapidly became a more finished watercolour (*overleaf*).

Here we found a cisticola which is common at high altitudes in this part of Africa. The Aberdare Cisticola is a large dumpy cisticola, and sits up like a Stonechat on the open grassy hillsides where there are clumps of giant lobelia, thistles and the big bushy heathers (*overleaf*). By contrast, the Singing Cisticola is one of the most widely distributed species in Africa, from The Gambia to Ethiopia, and south to Mozambique. Noisy little family parties fossick around in low vegetation, chattering and duetting, and flicking their tails and wings.

61

The Slender-billed Starling (*left*) at the top of the waterfall.

Aberdare Cisticola (*below*) – one of the more boldly marked of this brown brotherhood.

Aberdares. 10500' A.s.l
30 Dec 1990.

Aberdare Cisticola, on open grassy
hillsides dotted with clumps of a
bushy heather, giant lobelia and
thistles.
large and dumpy, much like Stout
Cisticola at first sight, but streaking
heavier and tail all dark, tips paler
Very narrow pale edges to dark
tertials
Underparts silvery white with dusky
suffusion at sides of cheek.
Chin white

Note – males edges to tertials a more singed
brown. Tail feathers have brownish edges
and tips.
Head a bit
richer and
darker. Streaks
noticeable on
centre of
crown

Aberdares, 10,500'
3o Dec 1990
Mountain Chat

Thin yellowish-brown eyering
— More pronounced below eye

Undaparts noticeably
paler and buffy,
somewhat faintly
streaked.

Very upright stance

Tail generally looks
quite short and narrow

Tail shows mainly
white below with
dark smudge at tip
and a bit in the
centre.

Quite marked pale brownish
edges to greater coverts

Head rather flat

Moorland Chats.

64

The bird I named the **Mountain Chat (*left*)** on the drawings from the Aberdares has been variously called the Hill Chat, the Alpine Chat and the Moorland Chat, which is now the official name. In fact, the bird correctly called the Mountain Chat, or Mountain Wheatear, is a South African bird. I think to call it a hill chat understates its preferred elevation – it was originally discovered on Mount Kenya in 1899 at 13,000 feet, and is one of the very few birds resident at such high altitudes. However, it is quite common in these alpine moorlands, although it has a tiny geographic range, being confined to this habitat on mountains in Kenya and Ethiopia, and also on Mount Kilimanjaro.

When birding has gone quiet, I take the opportunity to make drawings of landscapes and plants, partly with a view to using this sort of material in future paintings, but also because I enjoy it. The very common acacia (*below*) known as the whistling thorn or the black-galled acacia, is often a conspicuous feature of the vegetation in open country. The galls are soft and purplish when young, but as they become older they go hard and black, and are inhabited by ants, which bore the little round holes in them.

Mountain Chat,
Adult and juvenile
Aberdares. 10 500
30 Dec 1990

Stem dull grey-brown, galls a
bit darker but not shiny –
thorns dull white. Leaves bright olive

Acacia drepanolobium
Whistling Thorn
Naro Moru   6 Nov.

65

Naro Moru and Shaba

Mount Kenya in the early morning, from Naro Moru. 8 November 1983

About 80 miles north of Nairobi, and looking at the western flank of Mount Kenya, lies the attractive resort of Naro Moru River Lodge. We spent a week there, having driven down from northern Kenya, and I have a wry entry in the notebook which says 'went shopping in the local village but couldn't get bread, but will be able to survive without'. Later entries show that shopping wasn't a hugely rewarding pastime, but birding in the lovely surroundings certainly was. The birdlife here is abundant, and the river that runs quietly past, and gives the resort its name, was delightful. Now and again we were able to see African Black Duck on it, for this is often a shy bird and likes its streams to have plenty of cover. A bird I was pleased to be able to study here was the local turaco, Hartlaub's, which frequented thick foliage in the big trees overhanging the stream, and was usually first located by its call.

Away from the river and the trees, the open countryside, at over 6500 feet, is a complete contrast, and stretches from the flanks of the mountain to the Aberdares. Long-tailed and Jackson's Widowbirds flopped around, and the perky Northern Anteater Chats were everywhere. Amongst the smaller birds there were several species of cisticola – those tiresome brown warblers that are best identified by call – or habitat. The open plains were the haunt of the Wing-snapping Cisticola, so-called because during the rising and falling display flight, when he circles around singing, high in the air, he flaps his wings rapidly so as to make a little clattering noise. This is a minute little warbler, and a larger cousin is aptly called the Stout Cisticola. A third species of high elevations is Hunter's, a duller bird but very vocal. A pair made a loud trilling warble at each other which I wrote down with some imagination as 'tidlidi-idl-idl-whicheepu', which just goes to show that one should never try to do this.

Jackson's Widowbird.

Anteater Chats - Naro Moru
Srov.

wing fluttering and calling

The **Northern Anteater Chat (*above*)** is a common and easily seen inhabitant of open grasslands in the Kenyan Highlands, and what it may lack in the way of colourful plumage, it makes up for by being a cheery character. Usually in pairs or family parties, the birds often display by hopping about and standing with drooped and shivering wings, to show the white underside of the flight feathers. It is very much a ground bird, perching prominently on a termite mound or rock, but also uses low perches such as gates, fences or wires, and nests in termite mounds or earth banks. Northern Anteater Chats are quite musical, and like getting together in small groups to show off and sing at each other.

6 November 1983.
Hartlaub's Turaco in
the rain forest,
Mount Kenya

Turacos are always wonderful birds to see. They – or at least the green and blue members of this really ancient family – epitomise for me the avian guardians of African forests. Dressed in forest greens, they flash their unexpected crimson flight feathers as they sail across a clearing, and then bound up the big branches as if they were on springs, one after the other. They are inclined to examine you – an interloper in their leafy paradise – with an inquisitive craning of the neck, as if to get a better view, and although often hidden in foliage, attract attention with their raucous calls.

The bird drawn here was in the lichen and moss-encrusted trees bordering the Naro Moru river, and was done largely from memory with the aid of a few sketches. One feature, which I could not have seen well and of which I was then unaware, is that the outer toe is usually directed sideways or backwards. This helps the bird to get a better grip on small branches when it is foraging for fruit.

Hartlaub's Turaco.

69

I was very keen to go up Mount Kenya, but was doubtful about Billy Cooper's Toyota 'The Monstrosity' being able to make it, as the rain had been very heavy. However, we were assured by the people at the gate that the seven miles of road to the meteorological station at 10,000 feet was passable. Buffaloes grazed at the edge of the forest, and we had plenty of time to admire the huge and magnificent trees by the road, absolutely festooned with dripping tresses of moss, since going up was very slow, with the mud 2 or 3 feet deep. However, 4-wheel drive and 4.5 litres of engine worked wonders until the last mile, when it all got too much. Assuming that we had left all the buffaloes lower down, we parked, and then walked up to about 11,000 feet. At that altitude, the forest has petered out, and one is into a boggy, tussocky moorland studded with the amazing giant lobelias and giant groundsel.

One of the target birds was the Scarlet-tufted Malachite Sunbird, but we could only find the commoner Malachite Sunbirds feeding on the lobelias. The plants were interesting here, with violets, Alpine lady's mantle, a forget-me-not and something like hemp agrimony. Kniphofia (red-hot poker) was also common, and in places the bamboos were huge and luxuriant.

Before we got back to the vehicle, heavy rain came on, and the drive down was an experience best enjoyed in retrospect. Sideways all the way, alarmingly so when approaching a narrow bridge set at an angle over a ravine! At one point we stuck fast against a rock wall with the wheels in a deep ditch, and only some extremely strong German tourists, who rapidly became soaking wet men of mud, managed to free us. When we reached the bottom the sun came out.

Twenty years later we explored Mount Kenya again, in company with our friends the Coverdales, in order to find the exotic-sounding Scarlet-tufted Malachite Sunbird which we had missed before. This time, though, we approached from a different direction. Leaving Nanyuki, we drove north for about half an hour before turning off on to the track. We passed shambas and small-holdings – all very well kept – and there were long, long views down the escarpment to the north.

Soon we were driving through *Hagenia* forest, with some really large trees and *Hypericum* bushes. We lost the way, then re-found the track, and started a very long and dusty uphill and down-dale drive through *Protea* scrub which had been burnt down in a huge fire the previous year. It did not look promising. We covered about 10 miles of this, seeing the peak of the mountain at intervals behind the nearer rounded hills. The only mammals were a couple of eland, and some zebra and a steinbok. Moorland Chats were very common, their stubby tails edged with white, and Hunter's Cisticolas duetted in the bushes. Finally we came to a place where the *Proteas* had largely escaped the fire and were in flower, and at last we found the quarry. Not only that, but the commoner Malachite Sunbird was there for comparison, and I sat down and made some drawings of these elegant, long-tailed mountain dwellers.

Scarlet tufted Malachite Sunbird
Mt Kenya 3200m
9 March

Attitude when sunbathing

Scarlet-tufted Malachite Sunbird (*left*) .

70

Doum palms by the Vaso Nyiro River, Shaba 1 November 1983

Doum-palms by the Uaso Nyiro river at Shaba (*above*).

White-headed Buffalo-Weavers (*below*) are unmistakable and common birds in acacia country in eastern Africa, and are very noisy and sociable, with a great variety of 'squeeching' whistles, especially around their huge stick nests. They often associate with other birds such as starlings, feeding and running around on the ground under the trees.

Just over 100 miles north of Mount Kenya is the little settlement of Archer's Post, from where the northern Kenyan district of Isiolo is policed, and where in the old days the King's African Rifles had a headquarters. Lying to the west of this are the game reserves of Samburu and Buffalo Springs. To the east, a bit more remote from the tourist trail, is the Shaba reserve, where we had booked in for a week. Driving from Naivasha, we had looked in at Thomson's Falls on a very grey and damp morning, and for a long stretch before reaching Nanyuki there had been really heavy rain, and the road was extremely muddy. While slithering to and fro, and often sideways, we were able to notice tens of thousands of swallows migrating in the rain, but further north it was much drier, and the road became a white dust strip. The camp is in an idyllic spot, at the edge of the Uaso Nyiro river, set below palm trees. There was a drop of about ten feet from near the front of our tent to the river. On the first evening, while walking along the river, we came across a freshly dead croc, about half a mile below camp, wedged by the current against a small island, and soon discovered that these animals are a real danger here. The previous week, three girls from the local village were standing a yard up from the water, and a yard back, when a croc knocked them in, and one girl was very badly injured before she could be rescued. The river is the northern boundary of the Shaba reserve, and is very scenic, bordered with the beautiful doum-palms (the only branching palm), and with a background of rocky hills that glow copper-coloured in the setting sun.

Shaba. 2 November 1983
Spur-winged Plovers

The "Mreat Walk"

On the banks of the river, a party of **Spur-winged Lapwings** (*above*) were very noisy; one bird in particular was very aggressive, displaying at others in a hunched posture, with his tail depressed, stalking around and constantly calling, while the others stretched up and called excitedly. When they are breeding, these plovers can be very aggressive towards other species, chasing away smaller plovers and stilts.

Three **European Golden Orioles (*above, right*)** fed avidly on figs in a tree immediately in front of the tent. Two adult birds and a pale streaky juvenile were presumably a family party recently arrived, and were far easier to watch here than they are at home, where they are shy and often concealed in heavy foliage. They foraged almost like parrots, climbing sideways up branches, and twisting the head around to pull at figs. These birds, at the end of October, were quite early migrants, and were probably on their way further south.

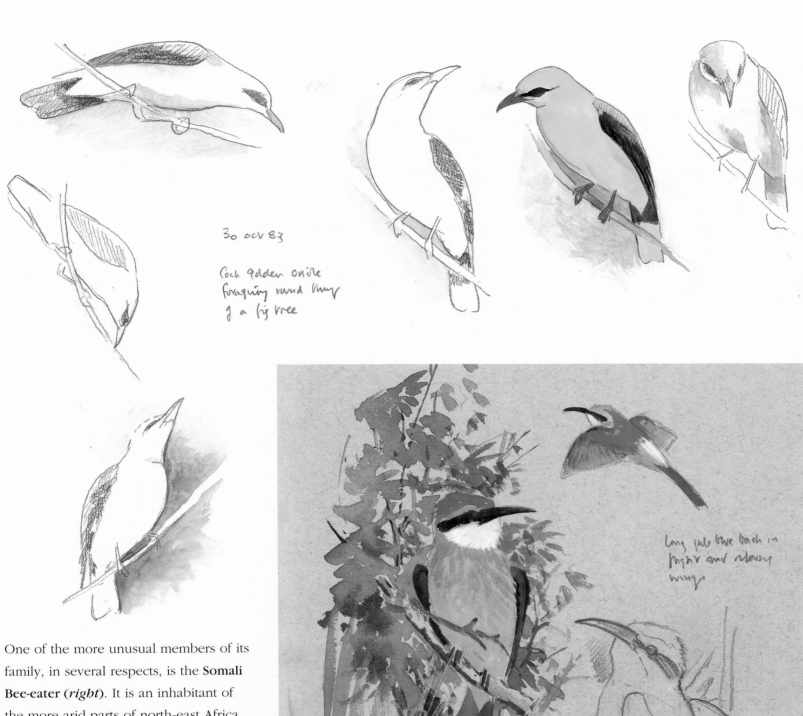

30 oct 83

Cock golden oriole
foraging round crown
of a fig tree

Shaba 1 Nov.
Somali Bee-eater. flew to a bush
and sat low down, with wings
lifted a bit - pale - head a bit large
& shaggy
Bill quite heavy

long pale blue back in
flight and relaxing
wings

One of the more unusual members of its family, in several respects, is the **Somali Bee-eater** (*right*). It is an inhabitant of the more arid parts of north-east Africa, and is a rather solitary and quiet bird. It somehow seems to lack the cheerfulness and joie de vivre of its relatives. One flew across the track and perched low down on the outside of a small shrub. A pale bird, almost white below, but with a shining light blue rump, it had a somewhat bedraggled or untidy look, with a large head and bill – indeed the bill looks particularly heavy for such a small bird – while the tail is quite short and narrow.

Shaba
3 Nov 83

Pygmy Kingfisher

Perching on thin lianas just in
front of the tent

better head & bill
proportion

One of the great advantages of sitting
still, drawing, or writing up notes, is
that birds often appear close by, and
do not have to be searched for. This
was the case with a **Pygmy Kingfisher**
(*left*), which came and perched on
some thin twigs just in front of the
tent, while I was perched less securely
on my sketching stool. A delightful
little bird, it sat looking around quite
unconcerned as I studied it at leisure.
The little pool in the path it was sitting
over was only an inch or two deep,
so I don't imagine it was thinking of
diving in, but could probably take
insects from the surface.

These studies of a **Sulphur-breasted
Bush-shrike** (*right*) were worked up
from quick pencil sketches as the
bird foraged around in a tree. Many
of the bush-shrikes have gorgeous
plumage, but are inveterate skulkers
in thick cover – this is a bird of more
open habitats, and can be watched for
longer than the usual microsecond.

Shaba
2 Nov 1983

Sulphur-breasted
Bush Shrike

Uaso Nyiro River, Shaba
1 Nov 83
Orange-bellied Parrot at
nest-hole in doum palm

A day exploring near camp had produced many European Rollers, and a party of four Cream-coloured Coursers, and we had a superb view of a neat little Pygmy Falcon, while amongst four-footed residents we admired many beautiful oryx, with their fantastic straight unicorn-type horns. Having nearly run out of petrol, we made a virtue of refuelling at the Samburu reserve by spending a day there, seeing much more animal life, and a party of eight Lesser Spotted Eagles. Somehow we acquired three locals who wanted a lift to Archer's Post, and then squeezed in an Italian and a Frenchman, and drove into a deluge. The track flooded, and so did the engine, but one of our passengers declared himself a mechanic, and dried out the points with a toilet roll we had just bought.

The combination of cruising gently around and stopping to draw had produced studies of the rather dull little Somali Bee-eater, an Orange-bellied Parrot that was nesting in one of the doum-palms, and a view of the river and palms. While I was writing up my notes and doing some drawing in the evening, the Tilley lamp attracted a cloud of insects, amongst which a huge and dozy rhinoceros beetle flew round incredibly slowly and silently, before crash-landing on the ground, drawing my attention to a scorpion running about. Just at that moment, one of the staff, in a great state of excitement, ran in to say he had just found a huge python in the kitchen. However, it had slithered off before we got there.

The charm of the Shaba reserve is that it is quite remote, and you can drive for miles without seeing any other people. One day we had gone some long distance from camp, and had stopped for a while to watch game. When it was time to go, 'The Monstrosity' absolutely refused to start. Three hours later, and covered in engine oil, we began wondering if our absence would ever be noticed, and thought about starting a fire to attract attention. (I once had to do this in the desert in Oman, but the trick is to wait until it is dark.) I banged the bonnet down in a temper, and climbed on to the roof to see if there was any chance of us being rescued (though there was hardly anyone in camp). I jumped down on the bonnet, and Barbara casually turned the key, and it started! Back at camp, dirty and hungry, I discovered that a lead to the battery was only connected by gravity, and looked perfectly in order until it was moved aside by a jolt. That evening, we were entertained by the reserve manager's father, who was now a big-game hunter, and took clients hunting. On one occasion, they had been following bongo in deep forest for a fortnight, and at last the client had one animal in the sights of his rifle. The hunter told him to rest the rifle on his shoulder and take aim as they crouched down. Instead of firing, the barrel began to wobble, and he saw that they were both covered in safari ants. Despite being urged to fire by the more experienced hunter, the client was quite unable to concentrate on the job in hand, and the bongo was spared, while the men had to strip naked to get rid of the swarming ants.

The Orange-bellied Parrot (*left*) was painted from a pencil sketch, not much impaired by the fact that I had to work by the light of a Tilley lamp, which was attracting a cloud of insects.

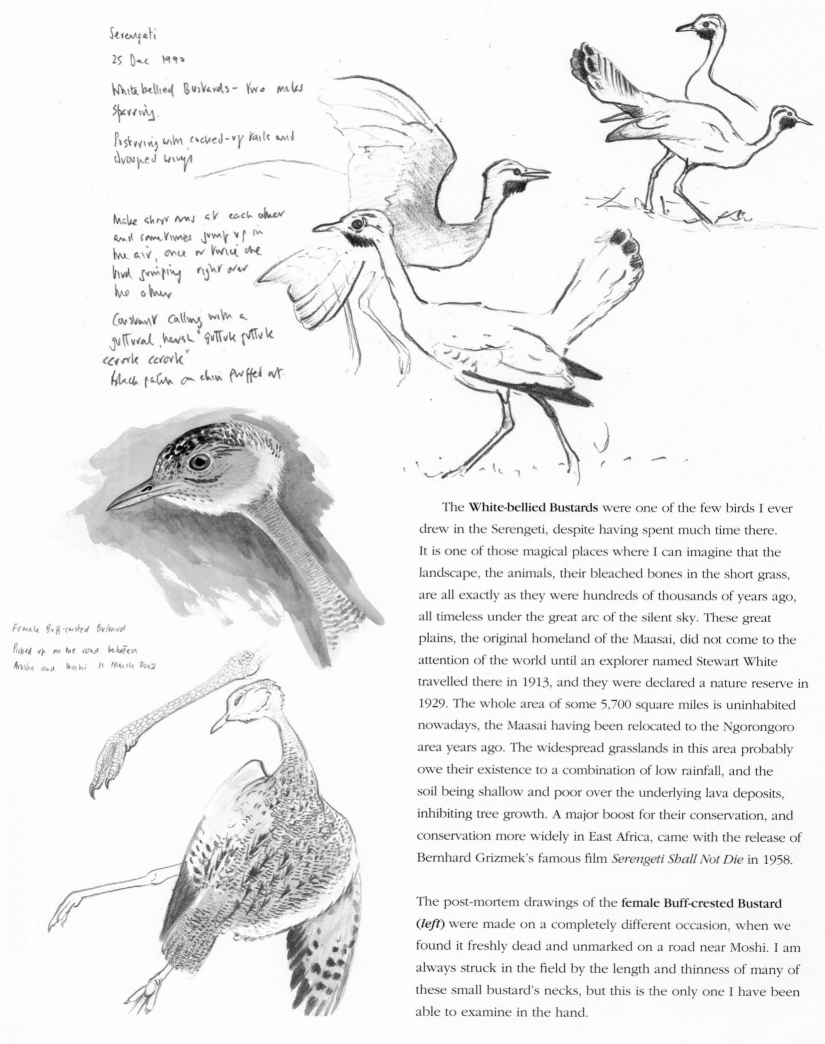

Serengeti
25 Dec 1990
White-bellied Bustards - two males
sparring.
Posturing with cocked-up tails and
drooped wings

Make short runs at each other
and sometimes jump up in
the air, once or twice one
bird jumping right over
the other

Constant calling with a
guttural, harsh "guttuk guttuk
cerork cerork"
Black patch on chin puffed out.

Female Buff-crested Bustard.
Picked up on the road between
Arusha and Moshi 11 March 2002

The **White-bellied Bustards** were one of the few birds I ever drew in the Serengeti, despite having spent much time there. It is one of those magical places where I can imagine that the landscape, the animals, their bleached bones in the short grass, are all exactly as they were hundreds of thousands of years ago, all timeless under the great arc of the silent sky. These great plains, the original homeland of the Maasai, did not come to the attention of the world until an explorer named Stewart White travelled there in 1913, and they were declared a nature reserve in 1929. The whole area of some 5,700 square miles is uninhabited nowadays, the Maasai having been relocated to the Ngorongoro area years ago. The widespread grasslands in this area probably owe their existence to a combination of low rainfall, and the soil being shallow and poor over the underlying lava deposits, inhibiting tree growth. A major boost for their conservation, and conservation more widely in East Africa, came with the release of Bernhard Grizmek's famous film *Serengeti Shall Not Die* in 1958.

The post-mortem drawings of the **female Buff-crested Bustard** (*left*) were made on a completely different occasion, when we found it freshly dead and unmarked on a road near Moshi. I am always struck in the field by the length and thinness of many of these small bustard's necks, but this is the only one I have been able to examine in the hand.

Pale loral area
o past back g eye

unstreaked
rufous head

breast + belly
greyish-white, flanks
thighs o vent + area
rich rufousy-buff

legs pale yellowish-brown

upperparts + tail
quite dark brownish
tail with indistinctly
defined darker tip

Rock-loving Cisticola habitat
Seronera 21 July 1987

One of the drawbacks of viewing the wonderful game parks in Africa is that, for obvious safety reasons, one is not allowed out of the vehicle. However, on one Serengeti trip, we went walkabout several times with an ecologist who was studying grass fires. Being out of the vehicle puts you very much on the alert, aware that a small inattention to detail can result in ending up as someone's lunch. Every bush is scrutinised not for the shrike on top of it, but the dozing lion behind it. I was not eaten on the occasion we went looking for a small brown bird

in the habitat sketched (*above*). The Rock-loving Cisticola is a bird with a marked aesthetic sense, for it haunts rocky outcrops from which there is almost always a fine view over the surrounding countryside. Why it likes large rocks is a mystery – no other member among its numerous family relatives does. It has also spent some hundreds of thousands – if not millions – of years searching out every rocky outcrop in Africa, and consequently has almost a continent-wide, though very spotty, distribution.

A Tanzanian lowland forest

Most of one July was spent in a forest in extreme north-west Tanzania at Minziro, west of the lake, and on the Ugandan border. The main object of our visit, masterminded and organised by our friend Neil Baker, was to search for central African species that might occur here, and which had not previously been recorded from Tanzania. The expedition included a number of people familiar with mist-netting, and I was keen to participate in order to study some of the forest birds that are difficult, if not impossible, to see well. As on other expeditions of this sort, not only was I able to draw birds held in the hand after they had been processed (ringed, measured and weighed), but I had a small cage into which we put amenable birds for short periods, when I could make more detailed paintings.

The party consisted of 14 people, including several drivers who doubled as cooks, and the arrangement was that the various groups, in their own vehicles, would rendezvous at Mwanza, a town on the eastern side of Lake Victoria, on a certain day, to take the weekly ferry across to the west side of the lake to Bukoba, saving a long, tortuous drive around the southern perimeter of the lake. Barbara and I had driven to Mwanza from Dar-es-Salaam in one of Neil's Land-Rovers with a Danish friend – Per Hirslund – taking a week for the journey.

From Lake Manyara to the Ngorongoro crater and the Serengeti, the landscapes and animals of this wonderful stretch of East Africa are the best example of how Africa looked when humans were beginning to evolve here about 4 million years ago. The most amazingly poignant trace of our earliest ancestors is the series of fossilised footprints of a family party, one of whom had turned aside to look back at something – maybe a volcano erupting. In stark contrast to the overwhelming scenes of wildlife we were experiencing, some of the birds I had made notes about on the way were spectacularly unspectacular –

a cisticola and a couple of pipits – but the journey was not without incident.

I was driving along a sandy track which ran through thick thorn scrub, when I saw, out of the corner of my eye, what looked like a long twig across the track. A moment later, voices yelled 'You've driven over a snake'. I said it couldn't have been a snake, it was too long, but I was overruled. I stopped in a small clearing, and in some apprehension, we looked behind the vehicle and all around, but there was no sign of the snake. We realised it must be in the Land-Rover, and decided to evacuate. This entailed jumping as far out as possible and running to a safe distance, and we could then see that the snake was hooked up on something underneath, with about a yard of it on the ground. All at once, we became aware of scolding birds in the bushes all around – many of them Silverbirds, attractive orange and grey flycatchers. How they became aware so quickly that a snake was under the vehicle was a mystery, since we had to get on our tummies to see it.

It was difficult to know what to do – we tried throwing sticks at it to get it to move – then I decided to jump back in the Land-Rover and drive a yard or two to see if I could dislodge it. When this failed, and we had spent an hour without getting the snake to move, we decided that it was stuck fast, and we should just have to drive on, in the knowledge that it might well be killed.

Eventually we reached the guard-post at the reserve exit, and were flagged down, as the snake had been spotted. It was now very battered and dead, but the guards extricated it – it had been injured in getting trapped on the axle or something. It was an Egyptian cobra, measuring exactly seven feet in length, and I was fined five pounds on the spot for killing an animal in a reserve.

Somewhat saddened, but glad there hadn't been a worse crisis, we motored on, and went to meet up with the others for the weekly ferry.

As we approached a roundabout in Mwanza, a figure leapt off it into the road, arms waving wildly. It was Neil. The ferry had gone the day before. There was nothing for it but to drive round the south and west shores of the lake. Arriving the next day at Bukoba, we found a town that was the very image of a colonial lakeside resort that had sunk into decay, and what had been fine old porticoe'd mansions were crumbling away. While walking by the lake, we were surprised to see, far out, what appeared to be a huge drifting cloud of smoke. Could there be fires burning along the shore, or what could it be? Minutes later, as the cloud drew nearer, we realised it was a hatch of lake-flies, which soon filled the air like aquatic locusts. They got into our ears, our eyes and noses, down shirt-fronts and I know not where else.

From Bukoba, we had to cross the border briefly into Uganda, and owing to the vagaries of African bureaucracy, had plenty of time to look at some local birds before re-entering Tanzania for the short drive to the outskirts of the forest.

Minziro forest, named after the local village, is a ground-water forest, in the Kagera region, and close to the river of that name, where I had stayed with Toni Nuti on her magical island 25 years earlier. It is in an area of extensive grassland which floods seasonally, and the forest reserve extends to about 65 square miles. We made camp at a previously reconnoitred site in tussocky grassland clearing at the edge of the forest, where a logger's trail entered. Conditions were quite damp when we arrived, with pools of water standing, though over the course of the month it dried out a lot. The tree canopy did not exceed about 100 feet high, though there were some isolated, very large, trees, including a huge *Ficus* about 300 yards along the path which was always full of hornbills, turacos, barbets and grey monkeys.

The clearing in the forest at Minziro (*above*).

For much of our visit, the weather was somewhat overcast, this being exacerbated later on when there was local burning of the grassland by villagers, and there was a very heavy dew in the mornings, so that clambering out of a small tent in long grass meant a damp start to the day. This greatly encouraged the mosquitoes, and anything left out by mistake at night was saturated. When the sun came out on a dull morning it transformed the scene – brilliant sunshine dappled the forest floor and lit up the clearings, and many butterflies – yellow and white and black and blue – took advantage of the warmth to emerge and flutter about.

A breath of wind would rustle the leaves in the canopy, though the stiff ginger lilies at ground level remained still. Big-leaved shrubs in the clearings swayed slowly, the sun glinting on their leaves. Later in the day the wind dropped, and the sky changed from grey-blue to dull yellow, and the tree frogs started their high-pitched 'teet-te-teet-teet' while the White-spotted Flufftail – a tiny crake – piped its repeated fluty note. The clearing resounded with the raucous calls of tree-hyraxes after dark, and dusk was the time for the Dwarf Bittern and the Bat Hawk. At this time, too, huge numbers of dragonflies hawked over the grass, but sadly had no effect on the mosquito numbers whatsoever.

As everyone who has birded in tropical forests will know, you only see a tiny percentage of the wildlife that you are seen by. Although perfectly well aware of this myself, the amount of time I spent, without success, trying to catch a glimpse of birds I had only seen in the nets, provoked this reflection.

White-bellied Kingfisher.

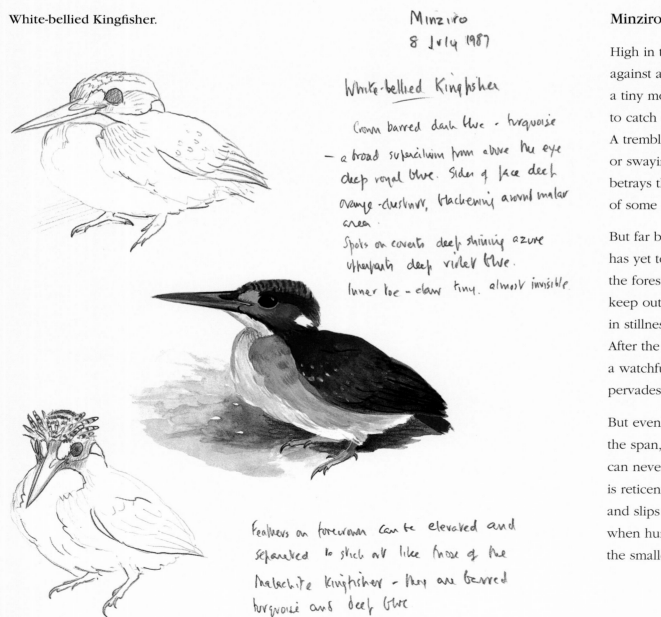

Minziro
8 July 1987

White-bellied Kingfisher

Crown barred dark blue - turquoise
- a broad supercilium from above the eye deep royal blue. Sides of face deep orange -chestnut, blackening around malar area.
Spots on coverts deep shining azure upperparts deep violet blue.
Inner toe - claw tiny. almost invisible.

Feathers on forecrown can be elevated and separated to stick out like those of the Malachite Kingfisher - they are barred turquoise and deep blue

Minziro Dawn

High in the canopy,
against a slowly lightening sky,
a tiny movement is enough
to catch the eye.
A trembling leaf
or swaying tendril
betrays the furtive passage
of some small bird or squirrel.

But far below, where light
has yet to penetrate and gild
the forest floor, a thousand eyes
keep out of sight
in stillness and in silence.
After the fading velvet night,
a watchful, wary calm
pervades the dawn.

But even by the light of day,
the span, the wealth of life,
can never be discerned,
is reticent to show its face,
and slips away without a trace
when human tread
the smallest leaf has turned.

Minzivo
14 July 1987

Blue-breasted Kingfisher
9 individuals netted, but
only one seen in the forest.

The handsome Blue-breasted Kingfisher (*above*).

The first task was to cut rides and erect mist nets. This involved much rough and ready 'gardening', people standing on other people's shoulders to get a suitable fix for the guy rope, and a certain amount of controlled chaos. A total length of about 400 yards of nets was erected by the finish, though as the maximum height was about 9 feet, we would be unable to net any of the canopy species.

Nets in forest reveal a fascinating insight into the lives of some of the birds, and how they obviously know their own patch down to the last twig. For instance, a small kingfisher, the White-bellied Kingfisher, (*opposite page*) was caught three times in exactly the same place in the same net, about a foot above the ground. This individual had a fixed route through the undergrowth, plant stems and so on, and kept on forgetting that we had put a net in the way. We netted 20 of these kingfishers during our stay, and it was a new species for the Tanzanian avifauna. A small, rather dull thrush, the Brown-chested Alethe, highlighted in dramatic fashion how impossible it can be to see forest birds when they are aware that you are in their home patch. No-one saw the species at all in the forest, though we caught many. Even a bird as brightly coloured as the Blue-breasted Kingfisher could be quite inconspicuous, since although we caught nine individuals, only one was actually seen.

Early on in our time at Minziro, four adult Forest Francolins were seen near the nets, again constituting the first record of the species for Tanzania. Soon, we netted what was presumed to be a young female (evidence of breeding now as well), and because of the interesting record, I made detailed studies of the bird. A week or so later, someone found a female at dawn, not far from camp, sitting twenty feet up in foliage in a tree near the forest trail. There was a sudden but silent and hurried rush to see it on the part of those of us who were awake. I looked at it hard, and went straight back to my sketchbook to draw it. (I did hardly any photography on these trips in order to concentrate on the birds better. In fact, on one four-month trip, I did not have a camera at all.) A couple of months later, back at home, we compared it with a snapshot Barbara had taken, and the drawing could well have been done direct from the photo, such was the

similarity. I had been tested severely on a previous trip, when I had drawn a couple of birds – a warbler and a flycatcher – and coloured them in water-soluble coloured pencils, a medium I used quite frequently. Neil looked at the drawings, and said 'Now what we'll do is put the nets up, and catch them, and compare the real colours with your effort!' This was a success on both counts, in that we did catch the birds, and I passed the test!

The female Forest Francolin sat on a branch at dawn (*below*) just long enough for me to memorise it, and go straight back to the sketchbook. Breakfast was hardly delayed at all.

Studies of Forest Francolins caught in the net (*right*) and held by someone while I drew them.

Minziro
14 July 1987

Female Forest Francolin

Mist-netted about 100 yards from the forest edge
above a burr above the ground -
four adults in a group with a juvenile.

One female seen early in the morning
roosting in a tree about 20 feet above
the path - see sketchbook.

The white markings on the underparts in the
female are broader, squarer and closer
together than in the male, so the underparts
look much paler.

Legs yellowish-flesh. Iris dark brown.

Forest Francolins

Minziro   July 1987

A rough colour study of the
female Forest Francolin.

Forest Francolin ♀
Miiiziro
July 1987

One of the more distinctive greenbuls
was this Green-tailed Bristlebill.

Mivizivo
18 July 1987

Green-tailed Bristlebill

Crown, earcoverts, upperparts all
dark yellowish olive, edge of
secs more pronounced indeed
humerus slightly wing patch. lower
edge of earcoverts and malar
area very dark brownish-green
almost black. No pale eyering
whatever. Around iris a dark
rim accentuating staring yellow
eye. legs - keer green with
purplish tinge. Sides of upper
breast tinged olive, also thighs.

Underparts from chin rich
lemon yellow, chin not different
from colour of breast - belly.
Tips of tail feathers a slightly
paler lemon yellow - perceptibly
so. Edge of forewing yellow
but not conspicuously so.
Lores slightly paler yellowish-
green than forecrown a
ear coverts.

Tips of outer 3 tail feathers
yellow. The 4th v. slightly
so.

Greenbuls are always a problem unless one is familiar with the calls, so it was always good to be able to handle them and study them in detail. One of the more striking species at Minziro was the Green-tailed Bristlebill, which has a staring yellow eye and yellow corners to the tail. It is right at the eastern extremity of its range at Minziro, as is its very close relative, the Red-tailed Bristlebill (*below*). This bird, however, has a dark eye that is accentuated by a whitish ring of skin around it, so while both species have a yellow throat sharply demarcated by dark sides, the appearance of the 'face' is completely different. In my notes I wrote the song of the green-tailed bird as a series of descending whistles, rather hoarse mournful notes, but Stuart Keith's descriptions in *The Birds of Africa* implies that this is in fact the song of the other one: it is sometimes difficult to be absolutely sure that the bird you are watching is actually making the noise you think it is. The acid test of this in the old days was to shoot the bird supposed to be vocalising, and if the song stopped with the bang this was deemed to be conclusive.

I watched a **Rufous Flycatcher-Thrush (*right*)** for some minutes as it sat singing, about 25 feet up, on the edge of a creeper. I made a nearly finished sketch, but helpfully we soon had one in the net, and I was able to work it up with more detail. In the end, we caught six individuals. I was able to copy this study, more or less exactly, for its portrait later in *The Birds of Africa*, though for reasons of design or a necessary comparison, it was rarely possible to do this. This is one of a group of four closely related species, two of which are more flycatcher-like than thrush-like. They sit upright, on rather short legs, and have a wide gape. The other two, called Ant-Thrushes – are also very similar, but one has a red tail, and the other a white-tipped black tail.

How these two pairs of birds have evolved is a mystery. They show pretty marginal differences, and yet the two ant-thrushes live alongside each other as good species across a wide area of west and central Africa, while one of the flycatchery ones lives in a small area well separated from the wide range of the almost identical Rufous Flycatcher-Thrush.

Minziro
15 July 1987

Bristlebill

The clean yellow throat is defined by the black malar area + lower ear coverts, and an dure wash across the breast, which extends onto the sides, the centre being clean yellow, a touch duller than the throat

Red-tailed Bristlebill.

88

Minzivo
10 July 1987

Eye dark hazel umber.
Legs, feet and claws
pale mauve-brown.

Rufous Flycatcher-Thrush
Stizorhina fraseri

Total length 7 in.

Wing 99
Bill 13·6
Tarsus 12·4
Tail 92   Weight 24·3 g.

6 individuals netted.

A bird was watched singing about 25 feet up
on the edge of a creeper. In this view,
the head does not look noticeably greyer
than the mantle except on the crown,
but the short wide bill was noticeable.
The song a repeated series of about eight
notes, like chip churp churp cheurp cheurp chip, declining at the end.

89

Immature female Tambourine Dove.
Minziro 15 July 87.

The small cage came into its own at Minziro, and putting in a few branches and twigs made a more comfortable environment for birds when they had settled down. It allowed me to make more finished watercolours of a number of birds, including two of the local doves, which are normally seen rocketing way from a path when flushed, or flying rapidly through the trees, and are therefore difficult to study closely. They are exceptionally beautiful at close quarters. **We caught the Tambourine Dove (*above*) and the Lemon Dove (*right*) in the nets on the same morning.**

MWWoodcock

Lemon Dove. Minziro. 18 July 87

Length 436 mm
Bill black, slightly tinged horn below.
Eye raw umber. Feet black
Forehead, crown, ear coverts, nape and the
whole back black with a slight brownish
tinge - a bit glossier on the crown with
brown shafts to the feathers. Primary
and Greater coverts rufous with 4 to 5
black bars about half the width of the
rufous bars, the coverts becoming progressively
blacker towards the inside of the wing.
The rufous and black bars alter in
proportion so that on the inside the
rufous is half the width of the
black barring. Primaries rufous for
above 7/8ths of their length with
blackish tips, and a certain amount
of black blackening on both the outer
and inner webs. The inner 4
or 5 primaries having up to 5 bars
at the tip, the inner ones having
barring all the way up the
inner web.

Secondaries blackish with a certain
amount of rufous barring. The tertials
black with faint buff tips. Chin
dirty white with a rufous tinge, the sides
of the breast pale rufous with whitish
shafts. The underparts are rather fluffy
and dirty white. Tail black with a
greenish tinge, faintly barred throughout
with very narrow pale bars. The underside
of the wing is largely light chestnut, almost
with a silvery sheen and the outer
primaries are barred underneath. On the
closed wing, the barring is conspicuous down to
and extending over the greater coverts, but the
primaries look more or less unbarred.

Juvenile Blue-headed Coucal
Mnzivo July 87
About 70% of life.

92

Miriziro
19 July '87

Black-bellied Seedcracker. ♂

Bill dark steel blue. Eye dark brown
legs & feet grey-brown.

Back and belly black, but a
browner line along closed
secondaries. Red of breast is
sullied with blackish feathers
legs & feet quite slender

The **Black-bellied Seedcracker (*above*)** was one of the more striking small birds, but I did not do too well with weavers here, and only have a note of having caught two Black-necked Weavers – a common forest species.

One of the more unusual species about which I was able to make extensive notes was a sub-adult **Blue-headed Coucal (*left*)**, and the largest piece of paper I had only allowed a study about three-quarters life size. I had previously found that the rather nice, heavy brown paper, on which I had done a sketch of the Forest Francolin, was not really suitable for watercolour, and this is one of the very few studies I made using pastel. It has a somewhat richer quality, which seemed to suit this big bird.

Coucals are birds which like to lurk about in reedbeds and marshes, and are usually seen flopping away through the vegetation when disturbed, so it was interesting to be able to handle one. They are a group of similar looking birds in the cuckoo family, but unlike the Common and many other cuckoos, are not parasitic. The scientific name – *Centropus* – is from the Greek words meaning spike-footed, referring to the long, straight claw on the hind toe, and at one time this bird rejoiced in the vernacular name of Spike-heeled Pheasant-cuckoo.

Minziro
14 July 1987

Spotted Greenbuls.

*wing flicking action when foraging and
also (?) when displaying to other birds
in the group.
The parties of 5 or 6 move together through
the foliage, following one another at short intervals
or on occasion all sitting together on a branch
- close side by side. wing flicking and
tail flicking occur when the birds are very
close together as well as at other times*

One of the more engaging greenbul species here was the **Spotted Greenbul (*above*)**. They are friendly and sociable birds, though since they are a canopy species, we were not able to net one. However, I spent some time watching them from below, when they appear almost pure white. They are quite active birds while foraging, sometimes almost hanging upside-down and peering under the branches. Once a party of about a dozen appeared, keeping very close together and quite low in the foliage. Up to four birds would sit pressed up against each other on a branch; one or other would raise a wing, or flick out a wing, sometimes both wings at once, and also flirt the tail. One bird raised the wing quite mechanically, first to one side, then to the other, keeping it slightly flexed at the wrist and flicking the tail at the same time. The group would split up, one following the other at short intervals between the trees, and then catching it up and pressing together again. This is another species right at the eastern extremity of its range in north-west Tanzania.

Another greenbul completely new to Tanzania, and indeed one that hardly even gets to western Uganda, was the Icterine Greenbul (*below*), a very small bird hardly bigger than a European Robin. We netted 16 individuals, and it was a great opportunity to study this bird, since it occurs alongside an extremely similar, but very slightly larger, bird called Xavier's Greenbul. We were unable to distinguish these species on song, since so little was known about their vocalisations, and it was often difficult to tell which bird was making which call or song – the same problem we were having with the bristlebills. Being curious, I looked up the meaning of the word icterine – also the name of a European warbler. Apparently the Latin word *icterina*, derived from the Greek *icteros*, was a bird of yellowish-green colour. According to Pliny the Younger in the first century AD in his *Historia Naturalis*, a person with jaundice looking at it was cured, though the bird died. However, I am not inclined to believe this story. Icterine is a nice name for yellowish-green, though; perhaps Winsor and Newton could use it for a new watercolour for bird painters.

Minziro - 6 July 1987

Phyllastrephus icterinus

Bill dark on culmen, commissure and most of lower mandible pale purplish brown. Eyes pale raw umber. Conspicuous black rictal bristles. Legs short and toes very small with well curved claws. Legs & feet pale mauve-brown, the soles paler, claws light greyish.

Crown, mantle & wings olive brown. A faint yellowish supercilium. Ear coverts a paler olive. Underparts yellowish suffused with olive across the breast and clearly defining the clean yellow throat. Centre of belly cleaner yellow than flanks. Tail browner and redder than upperparts. A tiny greenbul, not much larger – if at all – than an Akalat.

Icterine Greenbul.

95

Cossypha natalensis
Minziro July 1987
(Red-capped Robin-chat)

Various small birds which hopped happily around in the cage were all species which were quite difficult to get much detail on when they were moving shyly around in the forest. They included the pretty Red-capped Robin-Chat (*above*) and, once more, its close relative the Blue-shouldered Robin-Chat (*right*) and I drew this in several poses as it moved around in the cage.

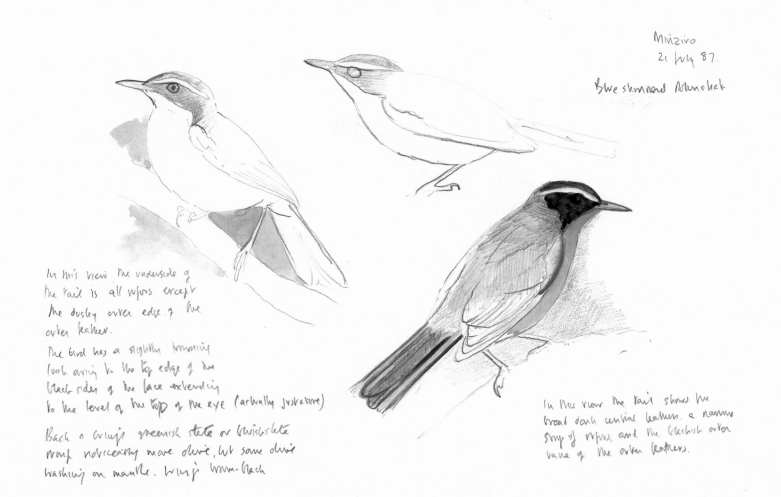

Miniziro
21 July 87.

Blue-shouldered Robin-chat

In this view the underside of
the tail is all rufous except
the dusky outer edge of the
outer feather.

The bird has a slightly frowning
look owing to the top edge of the
black sides of the face extending
to the level of the top of the eye (actually just above)

Back o wings greenish slate or mistletoe
noticeably more olive, but some olive
washing on mantle. Wings warm-black

In this view the tail shows the
broad dark central feathers, a narrow
strip of rufous, and the blackish outer
vane of the outer feathers.

Miniziro   Blue-shouldered Robin-chat
6 July 1987

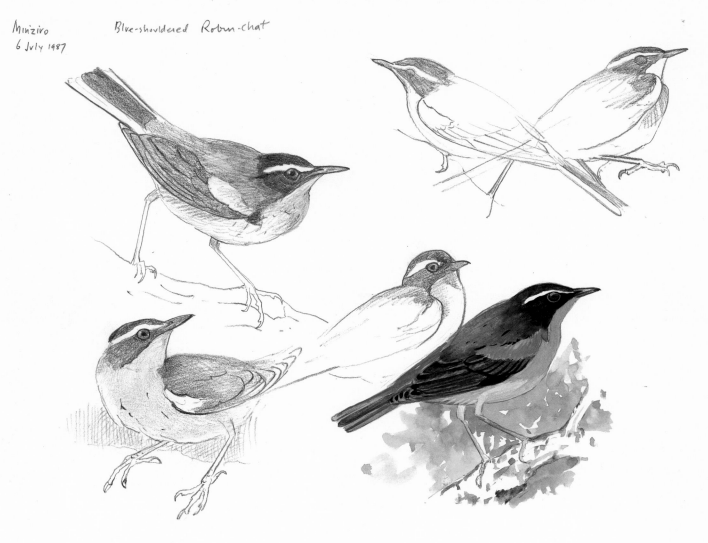

97

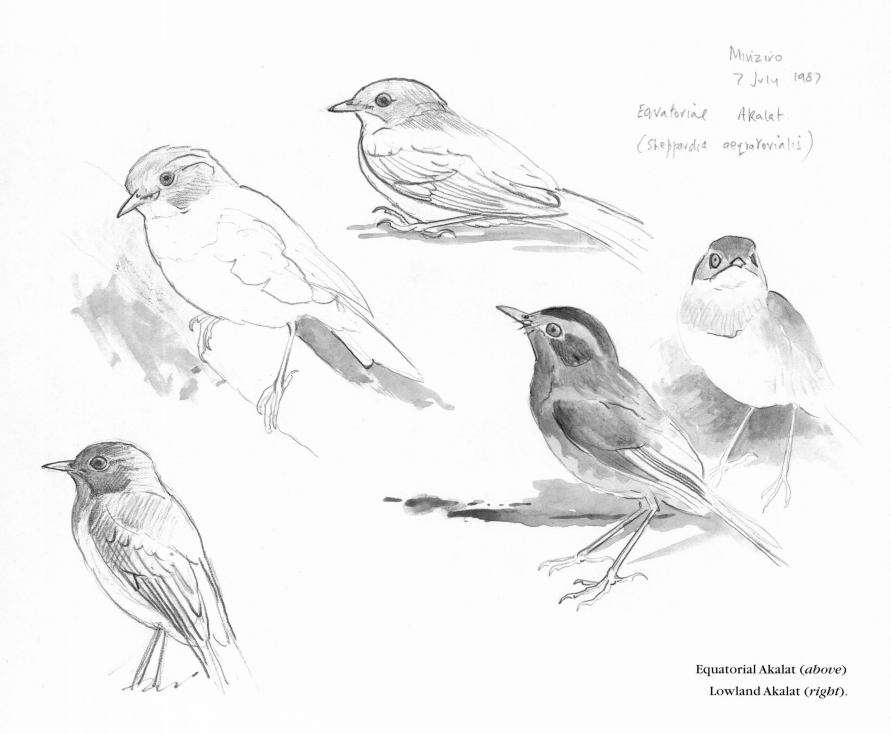

Miiziro
7 July 1987
Equatorial Akalat.
(Sheppardia aequatorialis)

Equatorial Akalat (*above*)
Lowland Akalat (*right*).

On this and subsequent trips, I became particularly interested in the small robin-like thrushes called akalats. The vernacular name comes from the Bulu name by which the bird – or rather the genus – is known in Cameroon. They are forest birds looking extremely like the familiar European Robin, though they are endemic to Africa. Most of the eight species have very restricted ranges within the tropics, and no fewer than six of them occur in Tanzania, two of these being endemic in the 'eastern arc' mountains, in the Udzungwas and the Usambaras.

The Lowland Akalat (*right*) is almost identical to the Equatorial Akalat (*above*) which I had previously seen at Kakamega, though is less rufous on the underparts. I made

a point of studying these birds, and the Lowland Akalat in particular, since this was a species which had never before been recorded in Tanzania.

It was while searching for birds a bit further away from camp, in the hope that the forest was less disturbed there, that Barbara and I got lost. We did not have a compass, and the sun was directly overhead. We went round in circles for an hour, often coming back to the same little pool, and eventually I climbed a tree to shout. The foliage was so dense it simply absorbed my voice, and the dust from it practically choked me. Later, someone heard us. We were only fifty yards from the path.

Lowland Akalat – much more extensive
white on the underparts than
the Equatorial Akalat

– Minziro July 1987

Juvenile Brown-chested Alethe.

Minziro
7 Jun 88

Brown-chested Alethe — juv.
Head breast and upperparts rich palish
rufous with dark feather edging giving
scaly appearance on back and rather
regular streaking on breast. Belly
paler-whitish. Bill dark brown, paler
at base of lower mandible and
gape swollen & yellow.
Legs pale mauve-brown. Eye dark brown.
Breast is lighter rufous than back.
Crown is dark brown speckled with rich
pale rufous. The supercilium of adult is
hinted at with a broad pale ring
of dark tipped, light orange feathers
round eye.

Juveniles of the small robins and thrushes are speckled just as in the European Robin, but they all differ to some extent, and are worth studying when they are netted. This Brown-chested Alethe (*above*) was netted close to the camp at Minziro. It is interesting that though this is obviously an abundant bird at low levels in the forest, the species was not seen once in the wild by any of the party, despite nine people spending a total of over 150 hours in close observation of the other forest birds. I suspect that, like many forest species, it becomes aware of strangers on its patch extremely quickly, and simply keeps out of sight. A small alert bird living a few feet above the ground would easily hear and see a human however quiet he or she attempts to be. I have sat for hours in some forests, knowing that some of these birds are there because they have flown into nets, and even then they refuse to show themselves. A particular problem for me in these situations is my poor hearing, which is a serious handicap in the field, so mist-netting is by far the most effective way of seeing the birds well.

Forest Robin

Minziro
6 July 1987

The colour on the imm. is much less clean orange, and the breast suffused with a huge of greenish-brown. Ear coverts and malar area jet black on adult. bur grey — a dark clean grey on imm. Imm. has crown slightly more olive than ear coverts. Upperparts on adult slate, on imm. a duller more olive slate.
Tail drawn too long on ad.

Imm. Note short tail. Throat and centre of breast only dull orange, flanks and underparts buffy. Wings a ringe browner than on adult, spotting on coverts almost invisible (pale tips almost worn off)

Sides of breast on imm. suffused pale slaty green. Legs — feet dull pale violet brown

Studies of the little Forest Robin.

I can't think why the Forest Robin (*above*) was called that, since all its close allies are essentially forest robins. It is a very small and short-tailed version of the akalats, and more brightly coloured, with a small white loral spot. However, unlike all the akalat species, this is a widely distributed forest bird, ranging from Liberia to Lake Victoria. Normally just as invisible as its congeners, it is most easily seen when, following a column of army ants, several birds posture and chase each other around.

Minziro
8 Jun 1987

Yellow Longbill.
Head & earcoverts grey -whitish on
chin to centre of breast
Dullish saffron-yellow on underparts
deepening on flanks.
Upperparts olive, greener on the
lesser coverts
Commissure + base of bill pale
yellowish. Eye golden. No eyering
or supercilium. Legs + feet grey
with a mauvish tinge.
Alula has a v. thin white edge.
Tail rounded. Some silky whitish
plumes sometimes project over
inner shoulder of closed wing.

There are five species in Africa, of which four are primarily west African, and the Yellow Longbill we netted at Minziro (*left*) was the first record for Tanzania, though it was known to occur nearby in Uganda. One of the species only occurs in a tiny area of Angola, and another, rather different from its congeners, is only in the eastern arc mountains in Tanzania. Though very vocal, longbills are not easy birds to study in their forest environment.

One of the other birds drawn at Minziro was the Green Hylia (*below*), an oddity among the warblers, apparently not having any close relations. It is largely a western and central African forest species that ranges as far east as Lake Victoria.

Minziro
20 July 1987

Green Hylia

Although we saw or netted about sixteen species of warblers in or around the forest at Minziro, I have few drawings of most of these, probably since I was concentrating on more unusual birds, and the warblers had no specific local interest. The little group of warblers known as the longbills, though, are a bit out of the ordinary, looking superficially like tiny greenbuls, with the long straight bills from which they get their name. They are also remarkable for the long, soft feathers on the flanks and rump, which can be puffed out, though the reason or necessity for this is unknown.

supercilium, forepair of earcoverts
& throat buffish yellow. Crown
& upperparts dark olive brown
eyestripe blackish brown. All
underparts dushy white. Tail as
Upperparts. centre of wing + Tail feathers
dark brown edged olive.
Legs + feet olive.
No pale ring around eye.   Bill relatively stubby

The yellowish supercilium and
face contrasting with the dark
crown and eyestripe, and the
dull greyish-white underparts with
a tinge of buff are noticeable
features. All dark olive above

102

Minziro
9 July 1987

Stonechat

African Stonechat.

The race of the Common Stonechat (*above*) in much of Kenya and Tanzania is an eye-catching bird of open grassy areas, much brighter than the familiar British bird in its breeding plumage. It somehow looks more exotic – in keeping with other colourful grassland birds like the ubiquitous Little Bee-eaters. Recent research suggests that it may, in fact, be a good species.

The beautiful Narina's Trogon is a difficult bird to see, but is not an uncommon species of African forests. There are only three members in Africa of this widespread, largely tropical family, with many more in Asia and especially the Americas, all sharing a similar general appearance. Solitary, and apparently indolent – spending much time motionless in thick foliage while on the look-out for insects – they are not easy to find, despite their bright colours, and it is always a pleasure to see one well. There were several sightings of Narina's Trogons during our stay at Minziro, though none was netted, since they usually foraged above the height of the nets. One afternoon, I had gone into the forest with my sketchbook to wander around and see what would turn up. After a while, I decided to sit down rather than move about, and chose a place where I had a clear view.

Mmziko
14 July 1987
Trogon

Studies of the Narina's Trogon.

After several minutes, I saw a trogon fly into a tree across the other side of the clearing, and perch on a small branch in full sunlight. At first it had its back to me, but then turned round to show its crimson underparts (*left*). I watched it for some time, making several drawings, before it noticed me, cocked its head, and looked down at me with each eye, alternately. It then disregarded me, and went on peering about for insects. It was shifting its position on the perch, turning round completely now and again, until, presumably disappointed, it launched off the perch, spread its wings, and swooped away into the foliage. I sat looking at my drawings, and then added a bit of colour from my miniature watercolour box, and thought about the Frenchman, Levaillant, who had discovered the bird 200 years earlier, and given it the same name as he bestowed on his Hottentot girlfriend, because he couldn't pronounce her real name. One wonders whether she was just a little bit indolent as well as beautiful.

The drawing of the Fork-tailed Drongo catching a fly (*below*) was made on a different occasion, but is shown here because both the trogon and the drongo perch quietly while on the look-out, and have a similarly agile and aerobatic flight when pursuing prey, often fluttery and swooping, though the black open-country drongo is much livelier than the brilliantly coloured forest trogon. Red and iridescent green seem to be common colours of forest birds, and turacos and pittas come to mind. There are two other African drongo species which are forest birds, but they are black too.

Fork-tailed Drongo.

Blue-breasted Kingfisher in the
12 July

On one occasion we caught two Blue-
breasted Kingfishers in the nets at
the same time, and they looked very
splendid when held up together.

7 July. Minziro.

Red-fronted Antpecker

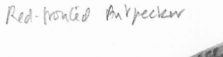

Diffuse dark scaling on edges of breast feathers

Flight feathers slightly darker than back. Tail similar the feet are strong, claws whitish legs + feet pale yellowish-brown — almost a dull yellow Inside of mouth pinkish

First record of the species for Tanzania!

Small groups of 2/3 birds seen in the forest. The bill is black and very slender - almost warbler-like, but with the nostril showing clearly. lores dark, and a round to the rear of the eye full crimson. Crown and all upperparts olive-grey, with the feathers on the crown just behind the red. patch dark-centred, with slightly yellowish edges. Sides of the face and all the underparts light rich rufous-buff, the wing lining paler, but a distinct pale ginger hue showing along the bend of the wing.

Wt 9.5 gr. wing 57 bill 10.5 tarsus 16 tail 38.

At the time we were in Minziro, there were thought to be two species of antpecker – members of the large family of estrildid finches – in Africa: the Red-fronted in West Africa, with a subspecies *jamesoni* in central Africa and Uganda, and Woodhouse's, also a central African species. We netted a single male of *jamesoni*, which was the first record of the species for Tanzania, but missed a great opportunity in not catching a female. More than ten years later, John Eyre, a sharp-eyed and knowledgeable ornithologist, was watching *jamesoni* in Uganda, but noticed that the female resembled that of Woodhouse's Antpecker. Fortunately, I heard about this shortly before painting these birds for *The Birds of Africa*. On checking museum specimens loaned from Belgium, I found that *jamesoni* differed sufficiently from the Red-fronted Antpecker (which lives thousands of miles away in Liberia and Sierra Leone), to be considered a valid species, now called Jameson's Antpecker.

One day I was walking along the path to a net-ride, past some rather thin and scraggy bushes that came up to my shoulder. Something caught my eye – I think it was the colour – and I looked down to see a vivid green snake looped languidly around the bush just by my left elbow. I think one reason people find snakes so unnerving is that they look you unflinchingly in the eye, but are completely devoid of expression. It is impossible to tell what they may be thinking, or what they are going to do. You know that, despite being as motionless as a statue, they can strike in a millisecond, like a coiled steel spring. Time seemed to stop; we were motionless, staring at each other as if frozen, except for that strange tongue, flickering in and out as if it had a mind of its own. My elbow was less than a foot from the snake's mouth, and I thought if

I tried to move quickly, and frightened it, I wouldn't be quick enough. I slowly and gently stepped backwards, and went to warn the others. We had a snake expert with us, and though he didn't recognise the species, knew that it was a back-fanged tree-snake and so, although extremely poisonous, could not have inflicted a lethal bite on a human. I didn't feel much calmer even on hearing that, and later learned that he may well have been wrong in any case!

More drawings of one of the Brown-chested Alethes we caught (*below*).

Overleaf – some quickly scribbled drawings of the little Forest Robin when I only had a pen with me.

Minziro
7 July 1987
Brown-chested Alethe
Back and wings more-chestnut
Crown greyer & ear-coverts grey.
Eye rather large. Legs long & strong
and a pale lilac-brown
Tail much blacker than upperparts

Breast is only faintly tinged
dusky and throat is not
well-defined except at
edge of malar area which
is dark grey.

Supercilium is white to over
eye and then becomes
dusky.
Primaries dark brown with
paler edges.

109

Primaries only project about 10mm beyond
longest tertial - tail rather short. The bird
is considerably smaller than the Akalat but
typically similar in posture, often standing
with legs well flexed or stretching up, and cocking
head.

Tanzanian tea gardens

Safaris in Tanzania with Neil and Liz Baker took us to a variety of places, and the diversity of habitats and scenery of this large country is immensely attractive, from dry coastal forests to miles of miombo woodland, to lush montane forests of the eastern arc mountains, salt lakes, remote game reserves and the high peaks of Kilimanjaro and Meru.

Through much kind hospitality we were also able to stay for long periods of time at Mufindi, a tea estate in southern Tanzania, and we owe much to our birding friends there, Johno and the late and lamented Kimbo Beakbane, and Alex Boswell, for showing us the local birdlife, lending us vehicles from time to time, and much else.

Mufindi lies in the southern highlands, at an altitude of around 6500 feet, near the southern end of the various montane blocks in Tanzania known as the 'eastern arc' mountains, which are famous for endemism in plants and birds. New discoveries continue to be made there, and not many people know that African violets are only found in the wild at the northern end of these mountains, in the Ulugurus and extreme south-eastern Kenya. A sensational ornithological find in 1991 was the Udzungwa Forest Partridge, whose closest relatives are the hill partridges of the Himalayas. It was discovered in a bowl of stew. It happened like this.

A party of Danish birders were camped in the forest, and, one night, noticed the feet of a gamebird in the meal their local cook had prepared. However, the feet were yellow, whereas other species known to live in that forest had red feet. A few snares were set by local hunters, and a pair of the partridges was obtained. They were not eaten, but caused a considerable stir since it was at once obvious that they belonged to a hitherto unknown species. Preserved as specimens, they eventually made their way to Gatwick, in a Dolcis shoe box, where I met the accompanying Danes, who had been alerted to my field characters (rather wild eyebrows at that time).

The partridges were handed over to me so that I could paint them, to illustrate the official scientific description in *Ibis,* the journal of the British Ornithologists' Union. It would be doing the Udzungwas an injustice if the painting of these iconic birds (*overleaf*) did not accompany this mention. Another new bird for the region was the Rufous-winged Sunbird, and other more recent finds have disclosed range extensions for a number of rare species.

One of the attractions of studying birds around Mufindi was that Liz and Kimbo had been mist-netting birds in the area for some time, and, once again, this proved invaluable for observing birds that otherwise would have remained a flitting blur in the poor light of the forest floor. There is much variety of habitat, since the tea gardens themselves are set amongst patches of indigenous relict forest, and there are streams and dams so that the tea can be irrigated in the dry season. The planted areas are interspersed with lines of eucalyptus, to provide firing for the tea factories. The Luisenga stream is a sparkling little jewel running through forest, alternately shaded, and then meandering through clearings.

There were other enticing localities nearby to visit, notably a wonderful lake at Ngwazi, with its reedbeds and waterbirds, and – a complete contrast – the largely unknown and wonderful game reserve at Ruaha. Here we were very kindly accommodated by the Fox family at Fox's camp, set amongst huge rocks on a small hill right by the Great Ruaha river. There is another game reserve at Mikumi, where we stayed from time to time, and further away across the mountains and down into the plains to the east, is the river at Ifakara, where a new species of weaver (*page 138*) had recently been discovered.

The Udzungwa Partridges; note the yellow feet, which were the items in the cooking pot leading to the species' discovery.

Mountain Marsh Widowbirds tangling
their tails in the blowing grasses.

Cishicola

Marsh Widowbirds — the cocks
flutter up from the grass with
widespread wings flaunting the
creamy shoulders — the tail
feathers mostly droop in flight
but when the birds settle
they get all bent and floppy
and curl in all directions
through the stems
The shoulder patch is a brilliant
pale creamy yellow and thin
yellow lines show (on edges?)
of tertials & some inner secs.

113

I spent a long time watching the Mountain Marsh Widowbirds amongst the reeds and long grass by Lake Ngwazi. The males were in full plumage, with full tails and shining creamy shoulders. They have a swaggering posture, holding the head well up, and often drooping and flaunting the wings as they sway on the tall stems, while the long tail feathers blow in all directions, and seem to flop around quite independently, often separated by grass blades or stalks. When the bird is flying, the tail droops out behind, but once amongst the stems takes on a life of its own. Many other birds were in evidence: pelicans, Spur-winged Geese, ibises, egrets, harriers and kites, while a Coppery-tailed Coucal foraged on lush grass near some bushes.

I was looking at an **African Darter** (*below*) through the telescope here one day and noticed that when it expanded the wings like a cormorant, the tiny feathers along the leading edge of the wing all stood up like little spikes. This was just after the bird had surfaced and perched following a long period submerged.

Ngwazi Lake, Mufindi

Immature African Darter

Note how all lesser coverts and alula are spiky and stand up quite separated while wings are expanded – this was following quite a long period mostly submerged.

13 Dec '83

Upper tail coverts tipped with red
Central tail feathers entirely red
all others red on outer webs except
outer pair all brown
Eye dark brown
Legs browny-yellow
soles yellow

Luhota Dam
Mufindi
11 Dec 83

Lesser Seedcrackers

Measurements from
netted birds –
Culmen 12·2
Depth at base 8·9
width of lower mandible
at base 10·00
Wing 61
Tarsus 18·1
Tail 55

Near one of the dams a new species for me was the **Lesser Seedcracker** (*above*), which I watched for some time before one flew into a net, and we could examine it in the hand. Near the same dam I noticed that a small thrush, the White-starred Robin, failed to live up to its name, because most of the time you can't see the white breast spot at all. This raises a problem for the illustrator, which also occurs with the bright pectoral tufts that sunbirds flirt when displaying. Often these are invisible, but to paint the birds in a reference work and not show these features is unsatisfactory, and putting them in may result in people thinking that they are a field mark, or that the bird always looks like that. It's either Hobson's choice, or being on the horns of a dilemma, whichever is most appropriate! Authors have the great advantage of being able to leave something out if they don't know it – or at any rate it would be better if they did – while the wretched illustrator has ten thousand people looking over his shoulder to see exactly how much he doesn't know.

115

We visited the Luisenga stream many times. It is an enchanting, small rocky stream, running down a thickly forested valley, and parts of the stream are in deep shade. In places like this, thick clumps of fern grow amongst the rocks on the bank and there are quite large tree-ferns. Big purple-and-black butterflies glide in and out of the dappled sunlight. Several times we were caught in heavy showers and were soaked as we pushed through tall grass and bracken. Birds were extremely difficult to see, the most obvious being Eastern Mountain Greenbuls and African Hill Babblers. However, it was a good place to put up nets, and the first time proved to be an exciting occasion. After a long walk, Liz and Kimbo joined us to go down to the Luisenga in the hope of catching the Iringa Akalat. We saw few birds, and returned to the house for lunch, where I drew Kimbo's Long-crested Eagle – 'Snaggle'. While I was doing this, the other three sneaked down to the nets and, lo and behold – there was an akalat! They brought it back in some excitement for me to study, so we put the little bird in a cage with twigs and bits of grass, and it behaved beautifully.

The sylvan Luisenga (*right*) here ripples from bright sunlight in to deep shade. Alfred, Lord Tennyson was a great one for streams and would have loved to see the Luisenga 'sparkle out among the fern/to bicker down a valley' and, even more apt, to watch 'the netted sunbeams dance/against its sandy shallows'.

Luisenga stream

Later, we took the akalat down to release it close to where it had been caught, and it hopped quietly out of the cage on to the path and began feeding on the ground two or three feet away. After birding for a while, when Liz had seen a small robin-chat with a white throat, we went to look at the nets. On coming to the first net we found a beautiful small bird in it – the black head contrasting with a white supercilium and a white throat – evidently the bird Liz had seen. While extricating it, another one flew into the net at the far end, but unfortunately bounced out. I was sure that the bird we had was a White-throated Robin, quite forgetting in the heat of the moment that they have black tails, whereas this bird had a bright rufous tail! Just before dusk, the second bird flew into the net again, and we decided to take both of them home for the night to identify them, seeing three pairs of Montane Nightjars on the way back as a bonus. I drew and painted the mystery bird, and a long look at Mackworth-Praed and Grant established that they were Olive-flanked Robin-Chats, but we had been puzzled because the illustration showed a much paler bird. Those illustrators!

We were up at five-thirty the next morning to release the new robin-chats near the stream, and opened up the nets. About an hour after dawn we checked them, and then had another surprise, finding another Iringa Akalat, and, with it, a beautiful Spot-throat. So we had caught three of the most elusive small thrushes, all with an extremely restricted distribution in Tanzania.

It is curious that such a rare bird as the Olive-flanked Robin-Chat has three distinct subspecies in Tanzania, where its total range only extends in a narrow arc along the mountains to northern Malawi, while there is a fourth race in southern Malawi and northern Mozambique. The two other birds are endemic to Tanzania in the eastern arc mountains. The Iringa Akalat, especially, is confined to the southern section, and is a quiet little bird of the forest understorey, and is very similar to the other small akalats, only rather duller, with much less orange on the underparts. Interestingly, in this respect, it is a half-way house to its other close relative the Usambara Akalat, which lacks any orange or buff, and has an even more restricted range to the north, in the west Usambaras.

The Spot-throat, the third rare species which lived in the undergrowth along the Luisenga, has a somewhat different structure and appearance, and indeed is now thought to be more closely related to the babblers rather than the thrushes. It has short and very rounded wings, but a broad tail, which is a very deep, rich rufous. I also noticed that the eye, which is surrounded by a dull whitish ring, is set well into the head, so that there is a bit of a brow, especially in a frontal view.

A few quick notes on the Iringa Akalat and the Spot-throat (*left*).

Mufindi – Luisenga stream.
28 Dec. 83
Iringa ground Robin

Netted in dense bush close to the stream – about a foot off the ground. Bill blackish-brown. Iris rich brown – no pale orbital ring.

Uniform brown involving llambs hw belly white. Throat pale russet, or greyish orange-buff, the centre paler and more yellowy.

Spot-throat

Eyering is flattened and broader at front & back. Whole back is a lovely deep olive, ringed brown.

Tail is broad, rounded and somewhat disintegrated. Wing very rounded, the primaries only a mm or two longer than the secondaries. Tail a deep rich rufous.

Both species show rather broad tails, the feathers with markedly ragged or decomposed edges but the Fan-tailed Warbler has much the broader tail, the more noteable because it is blackish. The initial appearance is almost that of a tiny coucal.

Mufindi
16 Dec '83

Cinnamon Bracken Warbler
(Just less than life size)

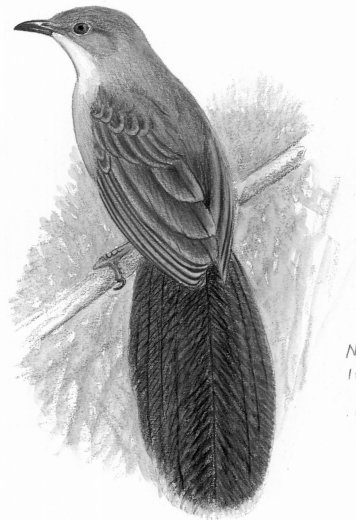

Ngwazi
18 Dec 83
Fan-tailed Warbler
(about life-size)

Fan-tailed Grassbird (*above, left*)
Common Bracken Warbler (*above, right*)

Two warblers that I wanted to study at Mufindi were the Cinnamon Bracken Warbler and the Fan-tailed Grassbird – the former being more difficult to see in dense low vegetation, while the other one frequents lush, long grass. In this habitat, with its broad tail, it almost looks like a tiny coucal. The Bracken Warbler was drawn first, from a bird which obligingly came up to the top of a burnt bush on the escarpment and allowed a good look for once, and both birds were re-drawn together from my notes and sketches.

Both of the two small warblers have large tails that are often quite ragged and disintegrated. One wonders why they need tails like this when they live in dense vegetation, which must cause wear. The tail on the Fan-tailed Warbler, as I called it then, seems in particular too big and heavy for the little bird, and droops as it flutters through the grass. The size of the tail is accentuated by being blackish. A newly adopted name for this species is the Fan-tailed Grassbird.

This painting of the Grasshopper Buzzard (*right*) was commissioned as a retirement present for one of the Mufindi estate managers. It was prompted by the studies (*below*) of a bird standing on the road.

Round golden yellow eye with quite small pupil. Wingtip nearly to end of tail. Primary coverts black man sees or coverts but with white tips. Tertials pale tipped and tail has pale tip and broad dark subterminal band.
When standing on road shows long legs like a harrier but Erite strong and thick.

Mufindi
10 Dec 83
Grasshopper Buzzard

Raptors are rarely seen on the ground close enough to make a considered drawing, but on one occasion a Grasshopper Buzzard was quite confiding, as is sometimes the case with these birds. When the wings are folded, the rufous patch , which is so evident in flight, cannot be seen. It is one of a group of four very similar birds, the other three being south Asian birds, and is an inter-tropical migrant, breeding across a wide swathe of sub-Saharan Africa. A southward movement after breeding takes it little south of the Equator, so this bird was at the very southern tip of its range.

119

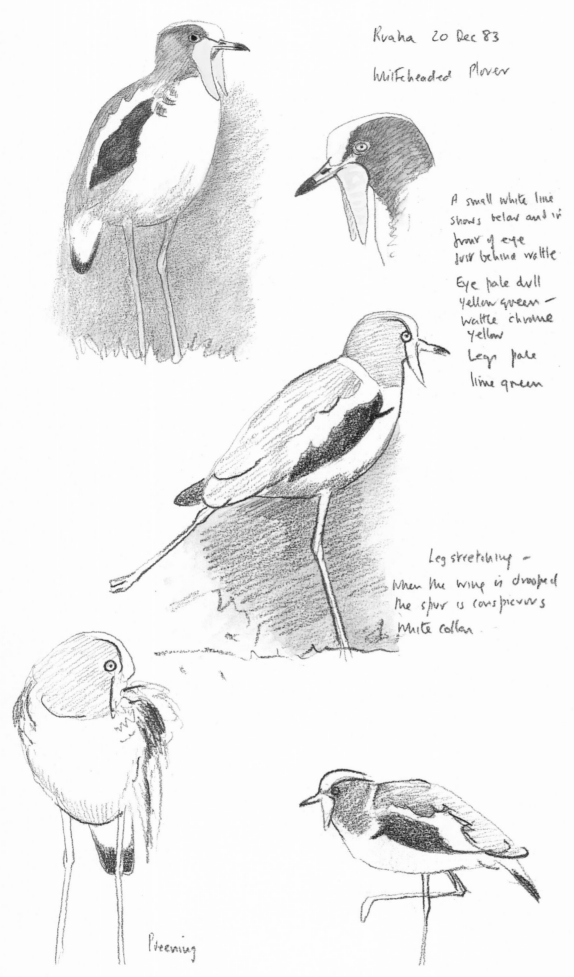

Ruaha 20 Dec 83

White-headed Plover

A small white line
shows below and in
front of eye
just behind wattle

Eye pale dull
yellow green —
wattle chrome
yellow

Legs pale
lime green

Leg stretching —
when the wing is drooped
the spur is conspicuous
& white collar.

Preening

While staying at Mufindi, an opportunity came up to spend several days in the Ruaha National Park, a huge and superb wildlife area, with Liz's sister, Christine. The drive from Mufindi, in Alex Boswell's dinky little green Daihatsu, took about six hours on rough roads. Amongst food we were taking to the Fox's camp, where we were to stay, was a basket of eggs, and on hitting one particularly large hole they were instantly scrambled. The Fox family had built a small game lodge in a delightful setting right by the Great Ruaha river. Several bungalows were scattered about a hill, amongst huge rocks that were as large as they were, or larger, and the hippos would come and look in at the front door. The only immediate drawback we could see was that we had to climb to the top of the hill to the dining room and bar. While we were drinking beer, a large solifugid (or camel spider) a fellow to which I have some aversion, climbed up Christine's back and got entangled in her hair. She was quite unfazed.

Both game and birds were plentiful, but one plover that I was particularly pleased to see was the **White-headed Lapwing (*left*)**, which has a small, patchy distribution in East Africa. Here they were by the river immediately in front of our bungalow, so I was able to make a few drawings. We drove many miles around this wilderness, though it was very wet at times, and we were glad that the Daihatsu could, on occasion, climb nearly vertical muddy river banks with no effort. Perhaps it was spurred on by the elephants just behind the exhaust.

White-headed Lapwing (*left*).

A study of one of the splendid baobabs at Ruaha (*right*).

Baobab Tree
Ruaha 21 Dec '83

Mbizi   16 Nov 90
Brownchested Alethe

ferrur pale arm
wash contrast with white chin

legs pale dull
pinkish claws whitish

Eye rich madder

More studies of the Brown-chested Alethe.

Four years after the expedition to Minziro, a similar trip was arranged by Neil Baker to the far south of Tanzania, to a forest at Mbizi, and though this was to be a shorter visit, we would be away for two months. The first ten days were spent largely with Miles and Liz Coverdale at the wonderful house they were then living in at Soysambu, on Lake Elmenteita. This was on the Delamere estate, and we drove around much of it looking at birds and animals. Thomson's gazelles were the commonest of the antelopes, about 8,000 being on the ranch, with many other species.

A further few days birding around Nairobi, and then we set off with the Coopers and Coverdales for Tanzania. A set-back occurred when Miles's Kenyan cook was refused permission to enter Tanzania, and had to be sent home on a bus, leaving us rather short-handed.

South of Arusha the country became dreadfully dry, and when we camped, hyenas laughed around the tents. It was no laughing matter when Liz woke up and found herself covered in ants. She was noisier than the hyenas, but worse was to come. Stopping for petrol, an unseen hand got into the vehicle as we were filling up, and removed Miles's briefcase, money, passports and all other documents. This wasted some hours before we could start again, and then it was a long slog through tall *miombo* forest on a narrow, winding track. We drove for hours (in fact, I think three days) without seeing anyone, and millions of tsetse flies were banging into the windscreen, as if we were driving through a hailstorm. We spent as little time outside as possible, but the tsetse were also unwelcome inside the vehicle, being practically unsquashable. It was a couple of days more before we were out of the woodland, and into wide open treeless highlands around Sumbawanga. This is an extremely unlovely town, and was reputed to be where unpopular civil servants were posted. I can't think of a worse punishment. We were told that there had been cases of plague there. We did not stop.

We eventually arrived well after dark in Mbizi forest, on an extremely narrow and bumpy track, which we could only follow in the headlights by guessing where another vehicle had broken through the vegetation. We assumed it must have been Neil, having heard nothing from him for a week or so.

The forest consisted of scattered patches of woodland on the relatively small hilly centre of Mbizi mountain, at an altitude of about 7,000 feet, separated by clearings with tall grass. The forest has a dense understorey, penetrated only by wild pig trails and the occasional stream. The campsite was at an altitude of about 6,600 feet, and although hot in the day from about 10 a.m. onwards, it became cool at night, and indeed cold in the wind. A Bat Hawk flew low over the camp in the early evening, in very purposeful, direct flight; the wings were a somewhat curious shape, being very pointed, but also broad-based. It was so close that the weak bill could easily be seen, and it was followed by a Brown-necked Parrot, squawking loudly. We had spells of torrential rain shortly after getting into the tent on the first night, and woke up to a deep grey morning, with cloud scudding over the trees on the hills. Soon another torrential downpour ensued, catching the campsite somewhat unawares around breakfast time, with no opportunity to fix tarpaulins securely, or put up new ones. People stood around in small damp groups, while torrents of water crashed off the tarpaulin above the kitchen area. For want of something better to do, I drew leaves by the kitchen with the water running off them. Apart from birding in the forest, where the nets produced many birds, there was plenty of opportunity to study the surrounding area, particularly the splendid open country on an escarpment overlooking Lake Rukwa.

Female Forest Batis

Mufindi
14 Dec 1983

The rich buff of the lesser coverts and the edge of the tertials sometimes makes a conspicuous kinked line down the wing.

Forest Batis.

Mbizi   16 Nov 90

Abyssinian Hill-Babbler.

legs slate green with
slight violet tinge
Bill greyish with paler
yellow-white tip lov
    v v pmv
eye dark red
No pale evering at all

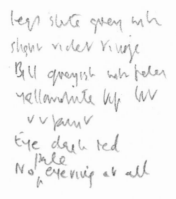

Lower flanks pale whos extending narrowly
up to axillaries. Underwing coverts white
All upperparts rich whos – centres of
tertials secs and primaries black
Coverts same as back Prim. coverts darker centred

Yellow-streaked greenbul

124

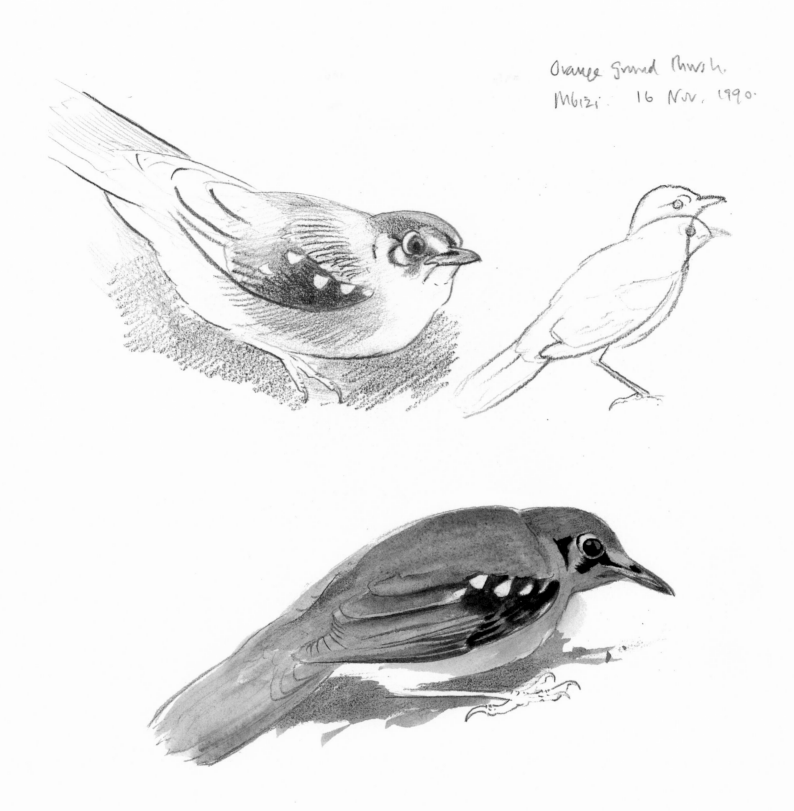

Orange Ground Thrush.
Mbizi. 16 Nov. 1990.

Small thrushes and greenbuls, and a fine Orange Ground Thrush were netted and drawn at camp. Another interesting little bird was the White-tailed Crested Flycatcher; it is only when handling birds such as this that one can appreciate details – the feet of this flycatcher are really tiny and delicate. Collared Sunbirds were particularly common around the camp, and seemed very bright – they were incredibly iridescent, and a deep yellow on the underparts.

An African Hill Babbler and a Yellow-streaked Greenbul (*left*) were some of the birds we netted, as well as a smart Orange Ground Thrush (*above*).

Eye bright umber
legs & feet light yellowish brown
almost dull raw sienna
Upperparts dull somewhat greyish
olive paler on underparts
Bill black
Head rather rounded - eye
looks relatively large
But short and stout
Eyering does not look v. obvious
in field .

Tanda 20 Nov 1990

Little greenbul

On a walk across the escarpment, we came through an area where there had been a grass fire, and the bushes were singed and brown. Foraging through these burnt leaves, I saw a pretty warbler, the Brown-headed Apalis (*right*), much of whose plumage reflected this burnt scenario, but with contrasting white, unsullied underparts, as if fire couldn't touch them. A couple of small warblers which I needed to compare here were the Cinnamon Bracken Warbler, already drawn at Mufindi, and the Evergreen Forest Warbler, each of which I tape-recorded, but getting good views as they skulked about in low vegetation was time-consuming.

A second camp was established an hour or so away to the south-west, in a beautiful spot at the edge of forest and near a stream, with open grassland and hills all around, in an area known as Tandam'buga, where there was a mosaic of *miombo,* grassland, swamp and groundwater forest. (M'buga is the local term for the slippery black cotton soil.) A pristine, unfrequented area, it was as if we had time-travelled, and landed in some pre-human African paradise. In fact, there was no village or settlement within miles. A feature of the grassland was the abundance of proteas, all in flower, and attracting masses of sunbirds – we counted twelve species immediately around the camp. Amongst them were the Copper Sunbird, and Anchieta's Sunbird, a particularly beautiful little bird, with a central scarlet band down the breast bordered with yellow. We cooled our feet in a limpid, quiet little stream, and were amused to find shoals of tiny fish nibbling in a very friendly way at our toes.

At dusk, we watched a Grass Owl hunting low over the ground between the proteas, quartering the ground like a larger and darker Barn Owl, though the facial disk is white.

In one of the bushy, wet clearings at the edge of the miombo woodland, a Rufous-bellied Heron flew over some tall grass by the water. It was a fine sight, the deep chestnut shoulder patches and slaty-grey back glowing almost crimson and purple in the bright sunlight, against a deep green background of the vegetation.

Brown-headed Apalis (*right*).

The ubiquitous and noisy Little Greenbul (*left*).

15 Nov 90.
Brownheaded Apalis
in bush with
an escarpment

Tanda
19 Nov 90
Moustached Warbler
orange-brown eye

19 Nov.   Siffling cisticola

A very large individual /race esp. tail
Wing 200 64
Bill 17·2
Tarsus 25·8
Tail 67
Wing tip to tail tip 46
↓

Tanda 21 Nov 1990

Redfaced Cisticola

Flat forehead -
marked gape line

Forehead raw sienna with
orange tinge - especially
on superciliun
pale in centre of lores
Reddish tinge on head
extends underneath on sides
of breast and more
extensively on flanks.
Mantle olive

Bill grayish horn upper mandible
pale pinkish-white below.
Eye clear raw umber
Legs and feet pink, claws whitish pink

Wing tip little longer than tertials

Tail slaty with olive
tinge of on outer vanes
v. narrow black subterminal
tip and buffy white
tips

Amongst the birds netted at Tanda
was the handsome Black-backed Barbet,
the possessor of a powerful bite, and
several cisticolas, amongst them the
Siffling Cisticola (*above*). Several years
later, I was discussing the derivation of
this name with Stuart Keith, one of the
senior editors of *The Birds of Africa*.
Amongst his many attributes, he had a
wonderfully dry sense of humour, and we
started inventing new cisticola species,
though the whining, piffling, wheezing
and sizzling cisticolas never made it in
the book. Quite enough anyway to have
to include winding, rattling, wailing and
croaking. Some of these names seem to
bring an elderly ornithologist in mind,
and I thought of old Admiral Lynes, who
made the definitive study of cisticolas,
whose vocalisations are often diagnostic.
Funnily enough, he was deaf.

**Some of the warblers at Tandam'buga.
Moustached Grass-Warbler (*top left*),
Siffling Cisticola (*above*), and Red-faced
Cisticola (*left*).**

Tanda
20 Nov 1990
Bocage's Robin

grey of crown
quite well
defined from
olive back

A bird which I would much like to have handled was the beautiful little Laura's Warbler, like a very bright lemon-yellow Willow Warbler – or perhaps a Wood Warbler, since the yellow breast contrasts markedly with the white belly. Though we saw one well at Tanda we could not catch it, since it was foraging at the top of a thirty foot tree. I did, however, study two grassland warblers in some detail, looking again at the Fan-tailed Grassbird, and the Moustached Grass-Warbler.

In the early morning, several Fan-tailed Grassbirds were flitting from one bush to another in an area of tall, wet grass, the wings making a short, whirring noise in the jerky, bouncing flight. Possibly this was some form of display, or territorial dispute.

Bill black. Eye very dark brown.
v. luminous

Very thin eyering hardly differentiated
from surrounding feathers but orange dots
below and pale brown above
Lores blackish but grey of crown comes
down to exactly ½ way behind eye
feathers above lores paler grey normally
but white when fluffed up
Primaries sepia contrasting with brown tertials
and secs
legs and feet grey with soles yellowish green

Another of the little robins netted at Tanda was **Bocage's Akalat (left)** which has an extremely restricted distribution, being confined to south-west Tanzania. It is interesting to speculate how this cluster of very similar species has evolved within a relatively small strip of isolated forested mountains in Tanzania.

Orchid –
Eulophia sp.

near Kihanga Dam,
Mufindi 18 Dec 83.

Following this excursion to the south, we returned to Mufindi, then had a short time in the Udzungwa mountains with Dave Moyer in order to look for more rare thrushes, in particular the Dappled Mountain-Robin. The song of this bird had never been recorded, and I had brought a good Marantz recorder with me for this purpose. Dave knew the song, so we sallied out from camp in a very wet dawn to try and see the bird and record it. I tried for two hours immediately after dawn in soaking wet conditions, with heavy rain and dripping undergrowth, to play back the song and try to encourage the bird to fly into the net. To say that it was elusive would be an understatement – it moved around like a will o' the wisp. However, we located one singing in very dense vegetation, up to about nine feet tall, on a hillside, with a stream and some small clearings nearby. I got quite good recordings, albeit with much background noise of Little Greenbuls and the rain, and we saw the bird several times in flight between the bushes, looking very rufous, and with very rounded wings.

At one time, it was singing vigorously against a Spot-throat nearby, which was standing in the rain on a small path, just at the same moment as two elephant-shrews happened to come out from the undergrowth. The session rather lost its charm when I caught my foot on a root while running to see the bird, and I fell heavily, bringing down a heavy shower of water, my binoculars and notebook going one way, while the tape recorder somehow hit me on the back of the head. Dave is the son of a missionary, and must have been taken aback by my language. Later, we had at least three Dappled Mountain-Robins flying around the nets, but they avoided getting caught. Yet other birds did not, and it was good to get a drawing of the **Spot-throat (*page 133*)**, and two more rare little robins, **Swynnerton's Robin (*overleaf*)**, and **Sharpe's Akalat (*right*)**.

That evening, sitting in the tent while the rain crashed down, we tried to tune in to the BBC World Service on a crackly old radio that kept going off station. We heard something like '…minister..Thatcher.. resigned …new Prime…John Major'.

We looked at each other and said 'Who?' and a political drama seemed totally remote and irrelevant.

130

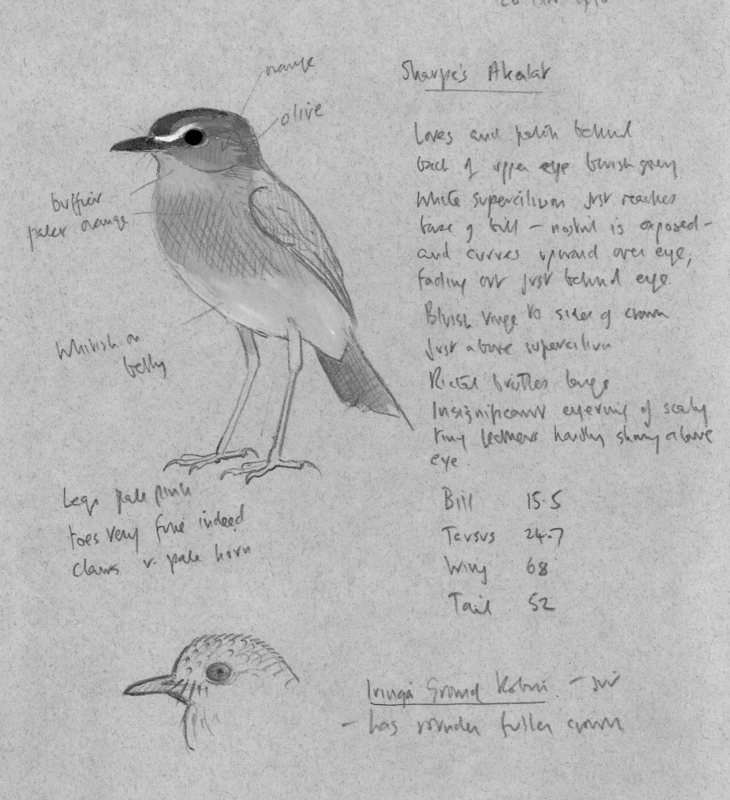

Uhafiwa
28 Nov 1990

nape

olive

buffier
paler orange

Whitish on
belly

Legs pale pink
toes very fine indeed
claws v. pale horn

Sharpe's Akalat

Lores and patch behind
back of upper eye brownish grey
White supercilium just reaches
base of bill – nostril is exposed –
and curves upward over eye,
fading out just behind eye.

Bluish tinge to sides of crown
just above supercilium

Rictal bristles long
Insignificant exposing of scaly
ring feathers hardly showing above
eye.

Bill   15.5
Tarsus   24.7
Wing   68
Tail   52

Iringa Ground Robin – juv
– has rounder fuller crown

Uhafiwa.
Uzungwe Mts

28 Nov 1990
Swynnerton's Robin

Rictal bristles not as pronounced
as in sharper Akalat
Pronounced though narrow white
eyering - not round but
flattened slightly on top and
rising toward rear
Crown brownish-olive, cheeks
somewhat paler and greyer
paling towards malar area
Throat white extending
to under eye accentuated
by dark collar which is thin
when head is hunched but
broadens in front when
throat extended
Bill long and thinnish

male

Female

Slate blue
wing

Below throat bright
Indian yellow with pronounced
olive brown flush on sides of
upper breast

Bill black
Legs deepish violet pink - claws horn
Feet very fine

Bill   17
Tarsus 25.5
Wing
Tail

132

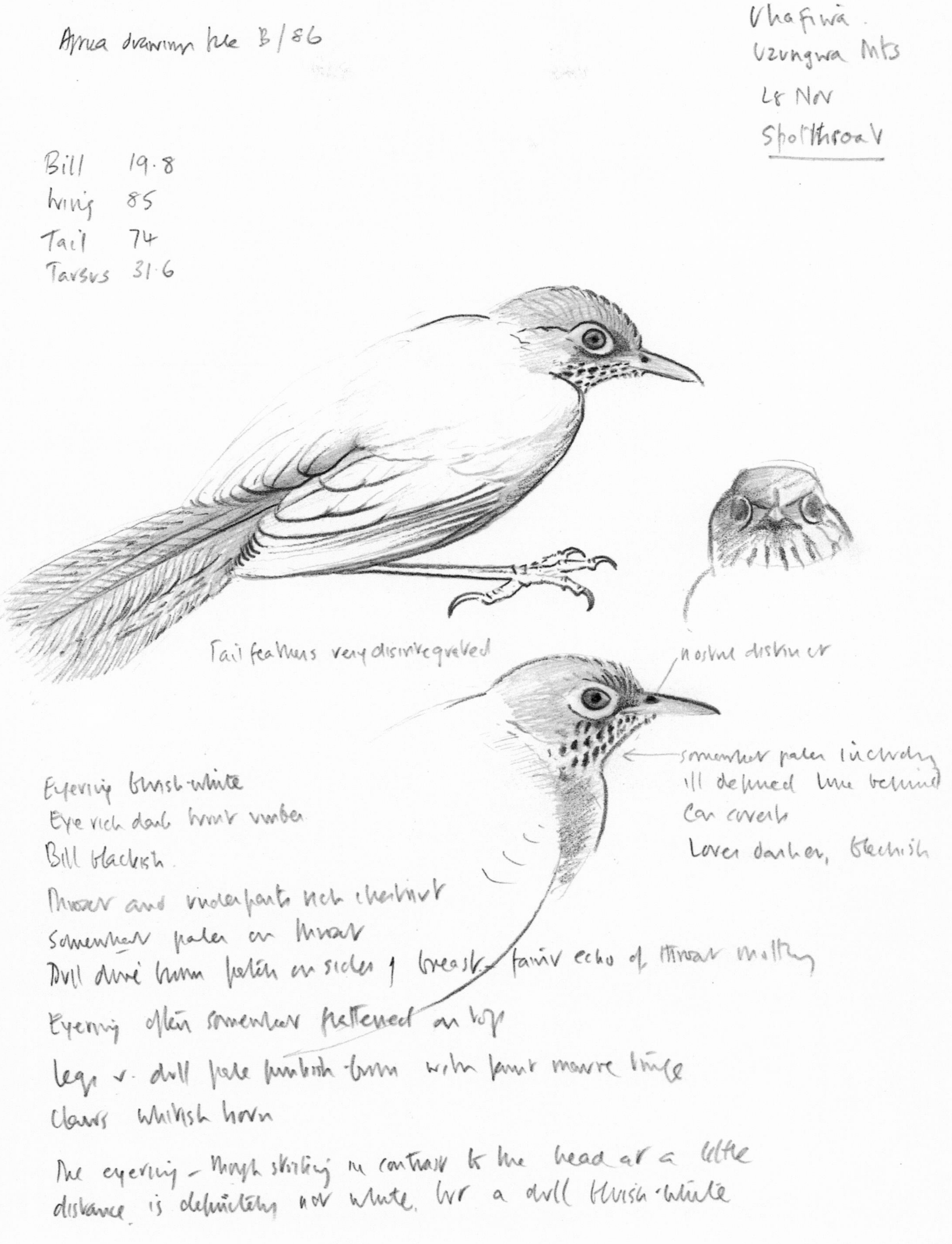

Africa drawing file B/86

Lhafiwa.
Uzungwa Mts
L8 Nov
Spotthroat

Bill   19.8
Wing 85
Tail   74
Tarsus 31.6

Tail feathers very disintegrated

nostril distinct

Eyering bluish-white
Eye rich dark burnt umber
Bill blackish.
Throat and underparts rich chestnut
somewhat paler on throat
Dull dark brown patch on sides of breast - faint echo of throat mottling

somewhat paler including
ill defined line behind
ear coverts
Lores darker, blackish

Eyering often somewhat flattened on top

Legs v. dull pale pinkish brown with faint mauve tinge

Claws whitish horn

The eyering - though striking in contrast to the head at a little
distance is definitely not white, but a dull bluish-white

Swynnerton's Robin (*left*) and **Spot-throat** (*above*).

133

The nest is made of green lichen and grasses, suspended 1 metre above the ground on a small sapling, on a hillside with an even but by no means dense undergrowth.

Nest of African Broadbill, Smithornis capensis, in forest in Udzungwa Mountains, Tanzania, containing 3 eggs. 28 November 1990

Amongst other interesting birds at Uhafiwa which I was able to study was the African Broadbill. We watched one displaying in dense forest. It was sitting about six feet off the ground, and every few seconds would launch off the perch and fly in a tight loop for a couple of seconds, making the loud, rattling display call. The white rump was exceedingly bright in the gloom, so the combination of the rump signal and the call served to make a small dull brown bird quite conspicuous in a dark, leafy environment. We found the broadbill's nest, made of green lichen and grass, and suspended on a small sapling about three feet above the ground. It was in forest and on a hillside where the vegetation was by no means dense. It held three eggs, and I made a careful drawing of it.

On the way back to Dar-es-Salaam with the Bakers, we spent a week in the Mikumi National Park, where I was able to get more drawing done in less demanding weather conditions. We were able to take advantage of joining Michael O'Meara on several netting expeditions, in addition to exciting viewing of animals and birds in the park. Amongst the raptors, Lizard Buzzard and Dickinson's Kestrel were seen well – my notes refer to both species having rather large heads. The Lizard Buzzard is a dumpy hawk, with legs that look as if they ought to be longer.

A pair of Red-throated Wrynecks were quite confiding, and we watched them for some time in an area where they had nested recently, and I was also able to make some drawings of **Arnott's Chat** (*right*). This is a southern and western bird in Tanzania, which we had previously seen in the great stretch of *miombo* woodland where the massed ranks of tsetse flies had made birding –or at least drawing birds – uncongenial. The cock – shown in the Mikumi drawings – has a white crown, so it was curious that in the *miombo,* a bird with a black crown was singing vigorously about 12 feet up in a tree, while close by there was a silent bird with a white crown.

Mikumi
3 Dec 1990
Arnotts Chat

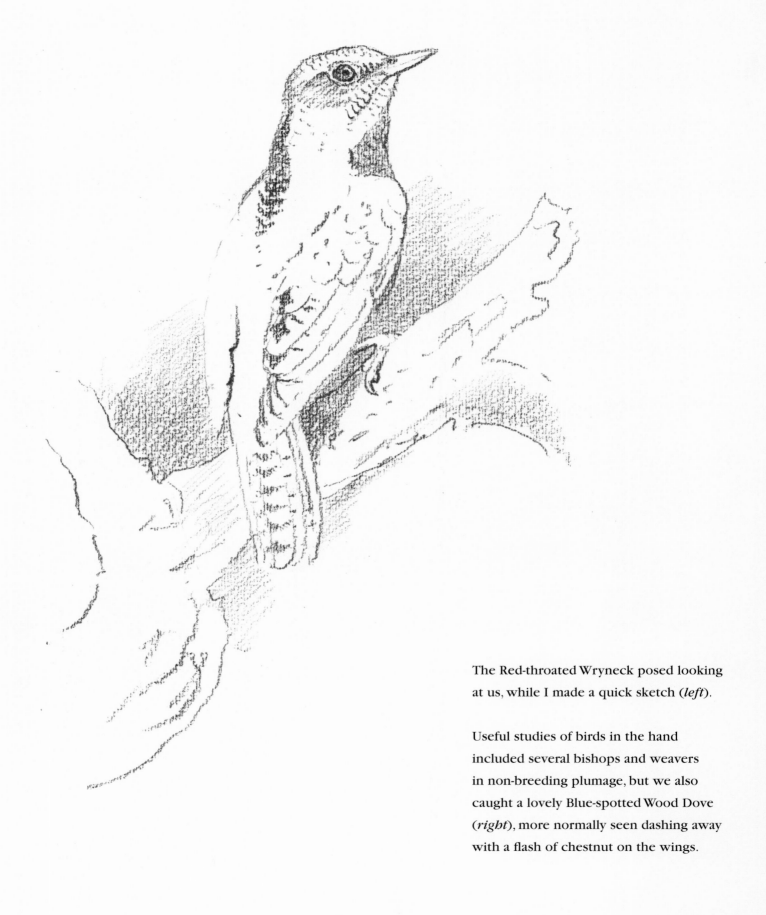

The Red-throated Wryneck posed looking at us, while I made a quick sketch (*left*).

Useful studies of birds in the hand included several bishops and weavers in non-breeding plumage, but we also caught a lovely Blue-spotted Wood Dove (*right*), more normally seen dashing away with a flash of chestnut on the wings.

Mikumi 4 Dec 1990
Bluespotted Wood Dove

Bill orange ⅔ tip, deep
maroon to base
Eye very dark burnt umber
Eyering minimal

Forehead whitish
shading to grey/lavender
crown, vinous pink on
breast

Primaries and primary coverts deep chestnut
tips and outer web near tip dark
brown. Alula black

We made an expedition from Mikumi across to the eastern side of the mountains, and down into the Rufiji flood-plain to a place called Ifakara, where a few years previously a Swiss doctor had noticed some weavers which he failed to identify. The Bakers recognised the significance of this, and it was quickly established that they were a new species, to be named the Kilombero Weaver, which I was able to paint for its formal scientific description. Having only seen a couple of skins, I wanted to look at the real thing. The birds were not difficult to find, though they seemed to be confined to a small area very close to the river, where they were in the reeds and hopping about on the bridge. Unfortunately, they were not in breeding plumage, but I was interested to see how small they were, with a tail that often looks disproportionately short and narrow. They seemed to feed mostly on the ground.

These Kilombero Weavers were painted from skins for the illustration to accompany the official scientific description in the *Bulletin of the British Ornithologists' Club*.

The weaver and bishop were drawn
from birds in the hand.

♀ <u>Masked Weaver</u>

Eye white with faint brownish
tinge.
Bill brownish pink somewhat
darker on upper mandible
and tip of lower.
Legs and feet dull
pinkish mauve.

Throat to breast bright lemon, also
yellowish wash on under tail coverts
Crown, sides of face, and mantle
bright yellow-olive. Mantle narrowly
streaked black. Coverts a slightly blacker
blackish brown with lemon edges.
Faint small dark smudge behind eye
Tail dark olive with very narrow yellowish
-green edges

(69-75)

Wing 74
Bill 12·9-15·8
Tarsus 18-22
Tail 46-55

largest and smallest
of 8 birds

Zanzibar Red Bishop ♂ non-breeding
plumage.

Upperparts cold pale greyish-raw umber
black streaks and feather centres
Supercilium white with faint buffy
tinge.
Bill dull dusky pink, paler on lower
mandible. Legs dull dark dusky pink

After arriving back at Dar-es-Salaam, we had intended to go on to the Serengeti for a week. However, the Land-Rover was not in a fit state to rove, so we arranged a trip to the Selous Game Reserve. This is a vast area, nearly as large as Switzerland at some 11,000 square miles, and much of it is difficult of access, so it is hard to know how effectively it functions as a reserve. It is named after the famous big-game hunter and naturalist Frederick Courtenay Selous, whose brother Edmund was a very fine naturalist, but confined his attention to English birds. F.C. Selous was killed by the Germans on the hills above the Rufiji river, near Beho-Beho, in 1917, in the First World War. He was serving with the Royal Fusiliers in the British force, then commanded by General Smuts, and it is amazing to think that he was personally leading his troops in an attack amid thick bush, at the age of 66.

We fixed up accommodation with a local guide called John Kasidi, who had a very small tented operation called Impala Camp by the Rufiji river. He was quite cavalier about the wildlife when walking around, and reassured us that there would not be any trouble as he carried a revolver! What was even more disturbing was that his driver, who went by the unusual name of Toyota, carried a rifle; any necessity to use that would have been truly scary.

I was very keen to see Pel's Fishing-owl (*left*), and persuaded John – I think against his better judgment – that we must do this from the river, as he had use of a boat.

Taking it down the river seemed a good idea at the time. It was a small boat, with an inch or two of freeboard, but the river was flowing in a pretty languid sort of way. Apart from nearly capsizing when I stepped into it, there was no immediate cause for worry, except that the engine took a long while to fire, and every time Toyota pulled the starter rope he had to recover his balance quickly. I recognised the symptoms, and strongly suspected that the engine had been removed from a McCulloch strimmer.

Pel's Fishing owl
Rufiji river 14 Dec.

On the Rufiji River

We were soon about a hundred yards out, and there were large numbers of inquisitive hippos whose snouts, just showing above the water, were higher than the sides of the boat. Some of them were very close indeed. Just then, the engine failed. We started drifting with the current, liable at any moment to shove an unwary hippo in the bottom. John got out his revolver. Toyota stood up to pull the cord. I started praying. Barbara was still calling out bird names. The river bank seemed a long way away, but I didn't like to turn my head to look back as it was destabilising. Anyway, we were now much nearer the far side of the river, where you can't go, and on the bank there were three surly old bull buffaloes. Just when I had abandoned hope, the strimmer fired, and we proceeded in a leisurely fashion downstream. John put away his revolver, and we steered in towards the bank, to inspect the large trees for the fishing-owl. After a while, I suddenly saw one sitting more or less out in the open on a huge branch. Although normally laid-back when seeing new birds, not to say taciturn, this was a real treat, and I leapt to my feet in some sort of ecstasy, precipitating an immediate crisis. The others jumped in different directions, so we balanced out, and with a deft bit of seamanship, Toyota brought the boat round so we could enjoy another look at the owl. It seemed completely indifferent, but I felt, all in all, it was a good tick.

Back at camp, I immediately made a sketch of the Pel's Fishing-owl sitting in the tree (*left*), and later worked this up into a more finished painting.

141

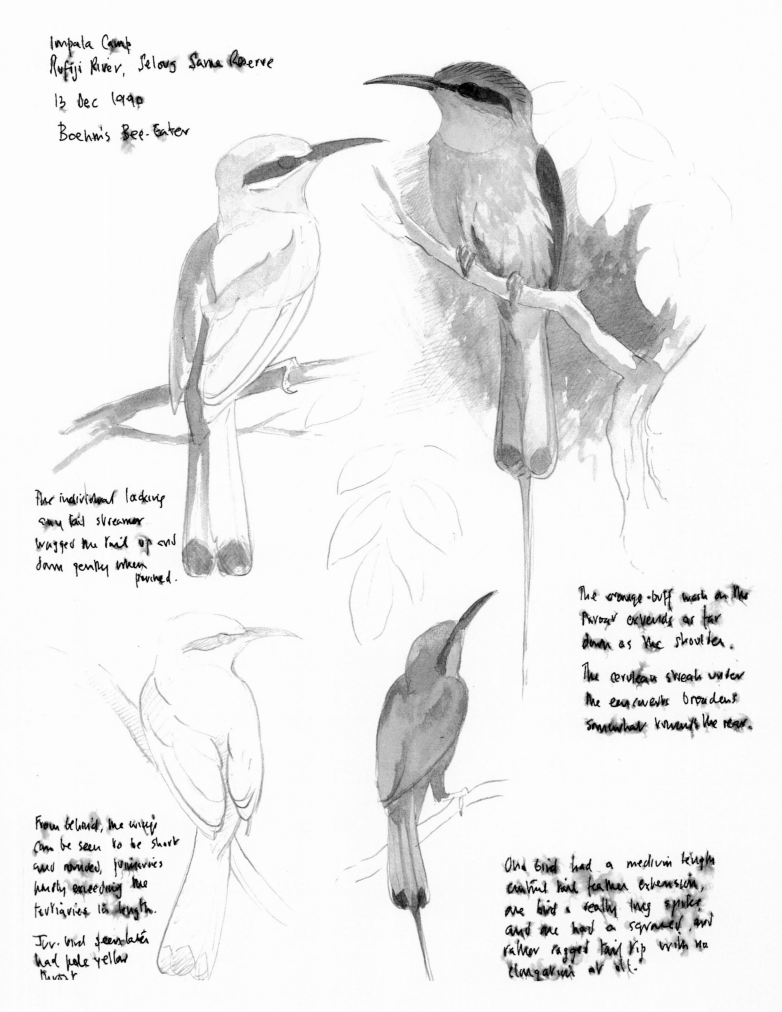

Impala Camp
Rufiji River, Selous Game Reserve
13 Dec 1990
Boehm's Bee-Eater

The individual lacking
any tail streamer
wagged the tail up and
down gently when
perched.

From behind, the wings
can be seen to be short
and rounded, primaries
hardly exceeding the
tertiaries in length.

Juv. bird seen later
had pale yellow
throat

The orange-buff wash on the
throat extends as far
down as the shoulder.

The cerulean streak under
the eye-coverts broadens
somewhat towards the rear.

One bird had a medium length
central tail feather extension,
one bird a really long spike,
and one had a squared, and
rather ragged tail tip with no
elongation at all.

Bohm's Bee-eater (*left*) and Carmine Bee-eaters (*below*).

Carmine Bee-eater.
Rufiji river
14 December 1990

insects, or sitting on trees and bushes. White-throated were especially numerous, the next in number being the somewhat confusingly named White-fronted, which has a very conspicuous red throat. Madagascar Bee-eaters, which we had noticed were lacking their tail streamers when seen around Dar-es-Salaam a week before, had fully developed tails here. The rather similar but prettier Blue-cheeked Bee-eaters were there for comparison, with their bright grass-green backs, and yellow throats shading to chestnut. A new and attractive species for me was Böhm's Bee-eater (*far left*) which only occurs in the southern parts of East Africa. Several were seen, perched in the lower branches of large trees near the river. Unusually for bee-eaters, they seemed to stay low down, often in quite deep shade. One lacked tail streamers altogether, and only a single bird hard really long streamers. While perched, the birds often wagged their tails slowly up and down. Out of all this throng, I only managed to draw two species, and I made the unusual mistake of annotating one of them in water-soluble ink. The drawing was out on the table, inevitably, just when a shower started.

Carmine Bee-eaters are arguably the most beautiful members of this delightful family. There are two races, Northern (*left*) and Southern, which lacks the greeny-blue throat. The range of the northern race extends across Africa from Senegal to Ethiopia, and our birds on the Rufiji river were at the southernmost limit of their non-breeding range. These bee-eaters are addicted to perching on large animals – more so than any others, from where they can sally out to catch insects, and will even hitch a lift on a Kori Bustard's ample back.

We did a good deal of birding on foot in the general area of John's little camp, safe in the knowledge that Toyota, who walked behind us, had the rifle. It was probably one that Selous left behind, and whether Toyota had any ammunition that fitted I know not. However, John still had his Colt. Bee-eaters were very numerous. No fewer than eight species enlivened the bush and skies, hawking around for

Rufiji River
Selous GR.
Dec 15 1990
Morning Thrush

often the collar is two almost parallel lines down the sides of the throat.

The Sombre Greenbul is a common bird in the bush, and not special in any way. I listened to one singing for a while when John's Land-Rover had broken down for the second time in as many miles, and in a resigned sort of way tried to transcribe the song into 'words', as an interesting exercise. I have always thought that this is a hopeless way of describing bird sounds, and eventually just put the song down as a short, dry, stuttering rattle, and felt much better.

The Collared Palm-Thrush (*left*) is a somewhat aberrant member of its family which I had not seen before, but they were quite common near the Rufiji. They stand up straight, showing a lot of neck and a rather small head. The Spotted Palm-Thrush, its closest relative, and a superb songster, was also quite common here. It was formerly called Spotted Morning Thrush.

Tail ample, often spread –bright orange-rufous.

Sombre Greenbul

Collared Palm Thrush (*above*) and Sombre Greenbul (*right*).

Ethiopia

Tississat falls
9 November 1995

E thiopia is a country of myths, legends and mystery – a shadowy realm shrouded in the curling mists of a great waterfall. Images are conjured by the press about the recurrent famines there as if it was all a howling desert, but in fact, no description of this beautiful and varied country can do it justice. It is noteworthy, as far as African birds are concerned, that so many have the word *abyssinica* as part of their scientific name. One feels that this must encapsulate the concept of being truly African, yet in so many ways the country that was Abyssinia, and is now Ethiopia, is quite unlike much of sub-Saharan Africa.

There is more to the history of this country than of the rest of Africa put together, with the exception of Egypt. It may have been the biblical land of Punt in ancient times, where ivory and frankincense came from, and was ruled by a dynasty supposedly descended from the son of King Solomon and the Queen of Sheba. It was under Jewish influence until the Ethiopian Orthodox Church – an offshoot of the Egyptian Coptic Church – was founded in the fourth century AD, but was then cut off from the rest of the Christian world following the Muslim conquest of Egypt in 675 AD. Contact with the outside world was not re-established for a further 800 years, when Portuguese Jesuits claimed to have found the kingdom of Prester John.

The Blue Nile plunging over the Tississat Falls, whose Amharic name means 'Smoking water' (*above*).

Tradition has it that the Ark of the Covenant was brought here after it disappeared from Jerusalem in about 650 BC, and it is said that it still remains here, its whereabouts a closely guarded secret. There is no doubt that some of the many monasteries contain ancient treasures, and all are adorned with paintings and frescoes of Saint George, the patron saint. The majority of the people are Christians, although there is a strong Muslim influence in the south.

As far as the geography and natural history were concerned, much was also a mystery, since the main river – the Blue Nile – was not navigable. In 1773, nearly 100 years before the source of the White Nile had been established, the explorer James Bruce had located the source of the Blue Nile, which drains the high mountains of Ethiopia and supplies most of Egypt's water. The seasonal floods, resulting from the rains here, enriched the Nile valley and enabled Egypt itself to survive. However, little was known for many years about the Blue Nile for the nearly 500 miles of its course before it flows into the White Nile at

Khartoum. The nature of the country had inhibited the sort of motorised travel that happened over much of East Africa in the first third of the twentieth century, and it was not until 1930 that the first plane flew over the Blue Nile valley.

From the naturalist's viewpoint, it is an incredibly rich and varied country, with many endemic species, and an almost unrivalled range of habitats, from the lush lakes and grasslands of the Rift Valley to the lowest and hottest desert on Earth, and some of the highest and bleakest montane landscapes in Africa. Lake Tana, at 6000 feet above sea level, spills down over the wonderful Tississat Falls to become the Blue Nile; the river then runs in a great curve through 400 miles of gorges up to a mile deep that rival the Grand Canyon, before joining the White Nile at Khartoum.

The number of endemic species of mammals and birds hints at the isolation of the country from a zoological standpoint. When its massive volcanic activity began to quieten down about 5 million years ago it must have been almost bereft of life, and even now the contrast between a fauna which is in many ways impoverished, yet high in endemism, is striking. The high mountains are home to a splendid antelope – the mountain nyala – as well as to an elegant long-legged wolf formerly called the Simien Fox, and the terrestrial Gelada baboon, placed in a genus of its own. A surprisingly large number of bird families have representatives that are endemic to Ethiopia, some of them extremely localised and rare. Among the commoner and easier to see species are a goose, an ibis, a francolin, a rail, a plover, a parrot, a starling, a chat and several larks.

Iconic species such as Salvadori's Seedeater and Prince Ruspoli's Turaco take a bit of looking for, as does the Ankober Serin, discovered only thirty years ago by the ornithologist John Ash, and living in a tiny area of windswept, cloudy fields above the Ankober escarpment.

Getting around is really only practicable by hiring a local driver and vehicle. Our driver did not have any experience of birders, and even less of some of the terrain he had to negotiate. He had a new 4WD Toyota, of which he was very proud, and winced perceptibly every time the sump found yet another rock. However, early on he was unaware of what was coming, and was jovial and interested. After three weeks of what was admittedly a rough ride, he declined to go any further, and we had to go back to Addis Ababa for a replacement.

Abyssinian Catbird in the British Embassy gardens Addis 8 Nov 95

The enigmatic Abyssinian Catbird (*left*).

Wattled Ibises (*above*).

Arrival in a new country always brings a tingle of anticipation, and one of the first surprises was the contrast between the modern city centre and the abattoir, to which we were heading. Addis Ababa is one of the highest capital cities in the world at over 8,000 feet. The pile of bones by the abattoir was not to be outdone, and was enormous – maybe 40 feet high – with an array of vultures and kites on it like a football crowd. On the rubbish-strewn valley around it, there were hundreds of Wattled Ibises (*above*), a disappointing venue for our first endemic species. Later, it was a relief to walk around the gardens of the Ghion Hotel, where the aptly-named Thick-billed Ravens were almost tame, and our third

endemic bird, the White-collared Pigeon, was common around town.

We had been given permission to walk in the grounds of the British Embassy – known as the 'compound ' – in fact by far the largest grounds of any of the embassies, extending over about a third of a square mile of grassy and wooded hillside. There was a good cover of indigenous trees where the Abyssinian Catbird trilled rather than miaowed. Whoever dubbed it a catbird must have known the rather similar North American catbird – no relation at all – but the fact that its real relatives are problematic is hinted at by its scientific name *Parophasma*. Roughly translated, this means a phantom tit-warbler!

Cliffchat at a church window
Lalibela

White-winged Cliff-Chat.

In the late afternoon, we flew northwards for a few days' visit to the country around Lake Tana and the Tississat Falls, where the Blue Nile starts to carve its way southward. This is open, partially cultivated countryside, and its fallow fields, rocky outcrops, streams and ditches were excellent for birds. One of the highlights was an enormous flock of hirundines – mostly Sand Martins – some tens of thousands of birds strong. There were also large flocks of local people wanting to act as guides around the falls, and even more so when we took a launch on the lake to visit a monastery on one of the peninsulas. Wonderful forest surrounded the monastery, with a closed canopy, and lush herb and shrub layers, but so many people clogged the narrow paths that serious birding was out of the question.

From Lake Tana, another flight took us to the ancient hill town of Lalibela, over some splendidly rugged country. It is only from the air that one can appreciate the deep sinuous gorges that rivers have cut across the plateau. We were surprised to see how extensively cultivated it was, with tiny homesteads and hamlets dotted about among the fields, especially as some parts are so remote and impossible to access that the inhabitants have not yet seen white people. The tumbled hunk of the Simien mountains rose on our left as the plane cleared a high ridge, with peaks rising above us on both sides as we came in to land. Lalibela is stunning, with its round stone houses in a dramatic rocky mountain setting, as well as its famous churches carved out of the rock below ground level. A spell of sightseeing is a must, but the birdlife is abundant.

The White-winged Cliff-Chat is a common bird around Lalibela, and one posed by a picturesque church window whose openings were carved in the form of a swastika. There are other interesting species, including the endemic Rüppell's Black Chat, and a distinct form of Mourning Wheatear. The open countryside is also good for buntings, seedeaters and stonechats.

The endemic White-billed Starlings (*below*).

White-billed starlings - Lalibela

white shine on the primaries
when they are drooped

Tail looks rather shortish and
a bit rounded.

Rueppell's Chat
Lalibela   9 November

when wings are tightly closed
no white shows.

Lalibela. 10 November
- *a black bird with a black shadow.*

Our guide suggested visiting a forest nearby, walking south from Lalibela over the beautiful undulating and open countryside. There were plenty of rocky ravines and bushed gorges with streams at the bottom, but not much in the way of trees. After about five miles we came to a small circular hut, proudly signed as the 'Queen of Sheba Tea-rooms'. There was space inside for at least three people, and we stayed for a cup of coffee. The only thing that wasn't actually necessary was to pick the beans, but the half-hour ceremony started with grinding them between two stones, and went on at an easy pace from there. There were several White-billed Starlings nearby, and a few other birds in a big olive tree. When the coffee came, it was delicious but tiny, and we judged it a good place to have stopped.

The forest turned out to be quite a well-wooded valley, and birds were plentiful – starlings, flycatchers, redstarts and others, and it was worth the walk just for getting the feel of the land. Near Lalibela on the way back we came across food aid being distributed in a huge dusty field, and the throng of white-robed figures had a strongly biblical appearance. This was also echoed on footpaths around the hills, where large robed figures practically concealed little trotting donkeys that kicked up puffs of dust.

The endemic Rüppell's Black Chat (*left, and above*), named after the great German ornithologist who explored this part of Africa.

10 November Lalibela

A noisy party of White-rumped Babblers

Eye reddish-brown

152

A rocky road near Lalibela

A hillside path near Lalibela (*above*).

We watched a noisy party of **White-rumped Babblers (*left and right*)** as they flew one after the other across the path – before they flew I had thought that they were the rarer White-headed Babblers, as all I could see was white heads among the leaves, but in flight the white rump is always diagnostic.

White-headed phase of White-rumped Babbler

Marabous standing around at the edge of the lake
while swallows flitter round them – Lake Ziwai   13 November

It could be a headline in a birding magazine or a tabloid newspaper: 'Menacing marabou swallows swallow' (*above*).

Back in Addis Ababa after a stay in the north, we picked up our driver with his new four-wheel drive, for the long journey south, past the lakes in the Rift valley, and then up over the Bale mountains, and down almost to the Kenyan border. Many of the lakes are huge, the walls of the Rift are far apart, and it was sometimes difficult even to see where the lake edges began, out in the dust and haze. At Ziwai, though, birding was easy, as there is a wide causeway running through a swamp to the edge of the lake, and pelicans, darters, and cormorants were quite tame, while plovers and Hamerkops ran about among the hoofed and footed traffic on the causeway.

Flocks of Barn Swallows circled and dipped around over the water's edge, and a group of Marabous stood stiffly, looking just like the bizarre birds in an Edward Lear cartoon. Then, suddenly, we had a nasty shock when one of the great birds suddenly snapped at a swallow flying past, and gulped it down.

On one of the lakes there were tens of thousands of Lesser Flamingos swimming along, and huge numbers of hirundines swarmed around the shores in a glaring heat haze. The lake is set in a basin of acacia woodland, where there were vast herds of goats and cattle. However, over-grazing has left the area a huge dust-bowl, and one wonders what there was left to browse.

Climbing up from the flat, dusty aridity of the Rift to the beautifully situated, and architecturally surprising, hotel at Wondo Genet was a welcome contrast. Here we came into lush forest, where jacarandas and spathodeas were in flower. Parrots and hornbills fed in a huge fig tree in the hotel garden, and a flock of Slender-billed Starlings perched along bare branches at the top of a tree, looking exactly like musical notes on a stave, with their quaver-note-tails hanging down.

Rouget's Rail, near Dinsho
15 November.
Habit of walking about on open stretches of short grass and flirting the white undertail coverts is more like a moorhen than eg Water Rail. It is a moor hen.

Silvery-cheeked Hornbill reaching for figs. Wondo Genet

Eastwards we drove across cultivated rolling plains and wide open spaces towards the foothills of the Bale mountains, having good views of the endemic Rouget's Rail (*above*), not one of your shy swamp dwellers, but something of a moorland moorhen. A lunch stop at Dinsho was memorable both for the décor – wallpapered from ceiling to floor with old newspapers, the very best food we had so far eaten, and the cost – 40p for three meals and three bottles of coke. The traditional Ethiopian meal, called *injira*, consists of a sort of large pancake that everyone shares, with a dollop of meat sauce of variable quality.

A Silvery-cheeked Hornbill (*left*) gorges on figs in the hotel garden at Wondo Genet.

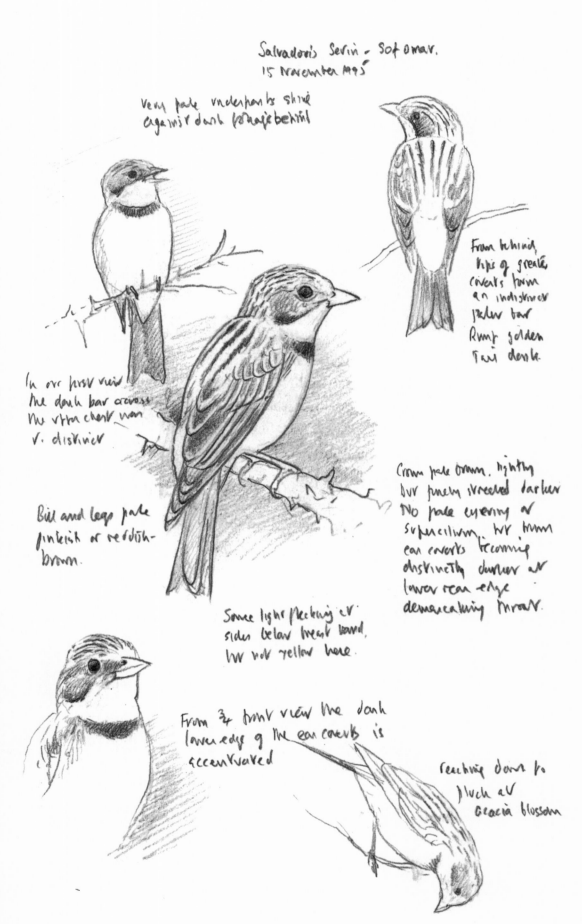

Salvadori's Serin - Sof Omar.
15 November 1995

Very pale underparts shine against dark foliage behind

From behind, tips of greater coverts form an indistinct paler bar
Rump golden
Tail dark.

In our first view the dark bar across the upper cheek was v. distinct

Crown pale brown, lightly but finely streaked darker
No pale eyering or supercilium. but warm ear coverts becoming distinctly darker at lower rear edge demarcating throat.

Bill and legs pale pinkish or reddish-brown.

Some light flecking at sides below break band, but not yellow here.

From ¾ front view the dark lower edge of the ear coverts is accentuated

reaching down to pluck at acacia blossom

An early start next day was necessary for the drive to Sof Omar to look for the extremely local and rare Salvadori's Seedeater, yet another of Ethiopa's endemic birds. Skirting the northern rim of the mountains, the road ran through vast fields of *teff*, a cereal like barley whose grain makes the *injira* pancakes. *Teff*, incidentally, is also endemic to Ethiopia. The seedeater lives in a very impressive gorge – so impressive, indeed, that we had to leave the vehicle at the top and walk down. There were parties of my favourite starling, the long-tailed Bristle-crowned Starling, in the gorge, and the bush was very green all around, the acacias in golden flower, and many trees and bushes in new leaf of yellow and orange. There had been rain only a fortnight before.

After nearly an hour, the seedeater was located by song, though it was at the very top of the tallest tree in the whole gorge. We watched it – just the one bird – for an hour and a half, and I was able to do some drawings. There were plenty of other birds of note – Shining Sunbird, Brown-tailed Rock Chats, a Grey Tit, Chestnut Weavers and more. At the end of the gorge we visited the entrance to the Sof Omar caves, an incredible system said to be nine miles long.

A sketch-page of Salvadori's Seedeater (*left*).

A day for the seedeater and then it was the big climb up into the mountains, through forests of *Hagenia* and juniper, where flowering shrubs bordered the clearings, and then higher, where scattered *Hypericum* trees – giant cousins of our familiar St John's worts – dotted the hillside with their glowing yellow flowers. Gradually, the trees become sparser and shorter, and at over 11,000 feet the plateau is a rolling, rock-strewn moorland, with great tussocks of some everlasting flower, and clumps of the endemic *Alchemilla haumanni*, looking very like our own lady's mantle. Thekla Larks ran among the stems of the giant lobelias, and a single Wattled Crane posed sentinel-like on a rock on the skyline. The plateau is honeycombed with the runs of root-rats, and when we stood quietly for a moment or two, there were soon lots of round, inquisitive little heads popping up all over. Big African hares were common, and galloped away with their ears sticking up. Around the pools, which were frozen in the early morning, and on ground white with frost, were Blue-winged Geese, pairs of Ruddy Shelducks, and parties of the endemic Spot-breasted Lapwings. Over one of the ravines we spotted a pair of Red-billed Choughs; the Ethiopian population, itself small and scattered, is the best part of three thousand miles from the only other choughs in Africa, in the Atlas mountains in Morocco, and not much closer to those in Turkey. The occasional Rouget's Rail appeared, and flocks of Ethiopian Siskins were common.

I felt that, in view of its rarity, the Salvadori's Seedeater (*right*) warranted a touch of colour from the paintbox.

Salvadori's Serin
Sof Omar   16 November

A group of Spot-breasted Lapwings
enjoyed the early sun by a small
frozen pool.

Spot-breasted Plovers - Bale mountains 17 November.

We drove up to the satellite station at nearly 14,000 feet, while an Augur Buzzard and a vulture soared above us, and on returning we came past a small gully where there was a dead donkey. An impressive array of raptors sat around on the rocks nearby, including a magnificent adult Lammergeier, whose mane glowed golden in the early sun. Later, a beautiful Ethiopian wolf sat dozing by the track, and as we stopped in admiration, it lolloped slowly up the hill, pausing only to make a lightning-fast 90-degree turn in mid-air to pounce on a rat, which it chewed thoughtfully before proceeding. Once called the Simien fox, it is much larger than our fox, though its brush was short and not very impressive. Curiously, it had two white lines down either side at the base, very noticeable from the rear.

We had an early start one day for the long drive over the mountains on the southward journey. As we came onto the plateau, the overall grey aspect was heightened by the frost, and a beautiful group of Spot-breasted Lapwings stood by a frozen pond waiting to warm up. Behind, much farther up the slope, a fine old bull mountain nyala trotted slowly away. This splendid antelope only occurs now on the Bale mountains, where it has adapted to what would seem to be a pretty meagre diet of dwarf montane vegetation.

The Ethiopian wolf (*below*) lopes away from the track.

Simien fox
Bale. Nov 1995

Mountain Nyala
Bale Mountains, Nov 1995

A bull mountain nyala (*above*).

At the southern edge of the plateau a great white cloud constantly rolled up over the edge and dissipated itself in the colder air, and as we began the descent, looking down on the cloud tops with fleeting glimpses of the plains below through the gaps, it was rather like flying. Soon we were in the thick of it, and the track corkscrewed down through dripping bushes and grass to the great Harenna forest, which ranges across the whole of the southern flank of the mountains. The part we crossed here was about 25 or 30 miles deep, and I would have liked to spend a lot more time here. Much of it has not been properly surveyed, and it is a stronghold of the lion in Ethiopia.

In places, the track crossed quite big streams, and the forest canopy and creepers arched overhead, but lower down the trees thinned and lost their stature, and then we were in a drier, rocky country of rolling hills and dense acacia bush. It was, in fact, rather too rocky a road for our cautious driver, who was very conscious of the knocks his precious vehicle was taking. It went on for some 80 miles, and was uncomfortable in several senses. This was a very sparsely populated area, and we saw only a handful of people after leaving the high plateau. Golden-breasted Starlings flew across the track, and when we came to an area studded with tall, red termite mounds, Red-and-yellow Barbets were common.

In about 1893 an Italian nobleman named Prince Ruspoli, with a penchant for exploration, came this way and collected a turaco that was new to science, and later named after him. The prince himself was unfortunately collected shortly afterwards by an elephant, and left few details as to where the bird had been. However, subsequent enquiry had discovered its haunts and we went to look for it.

Near a village called Wadera there is an area of short grass, as neat and green as the South Downs, with big clumps of bushes here and there, where there were many birds. There were also some very large juniper trees, and I happened to see a turaco flying along towards them. We scrambled down into a little valley with a stream and several well-spaced large trees. Three turacos appeared, and gave us excellent views; one flew on, but we watched the other two for another half an hour. We had almost forgotten the prince.

Wadera
14 November

Prince Ruspoli Turacos – a single bird flew
into the trees, followed by two more –
then the first one flew on up the valley
and the other two stayed around for
half an hour or so –

A couple of Prince Ruspoli's Turacos (*right*), one of Ethiopa's more colourful endemic birds.

Next day started badly with a search for the Degodi Lark, which proved to be a will-o'-the-wisp, at least as far as we were concerned, despite us being in the area in which it was supposed to occur. As I was transcribing this account from my journal, I learned that this bird has been found to be identical with a much commoner species called Gillett's Lark, which we did see in many places. I am very glad I didn't make extensive notes and sketches on the differences between the two supposed species.

Another long drive through the bush had left our driver punch-drunk, especially after he had had to cope with a split radiator. At a small village he carelessly drove through the rope at a road barrier, breaking it. The guards, already nervy after the village clinic had just been destroyed by dissidents, waved their Kalashnikovs menacingly at us, and we were on the point of

being the focus of an international incident when things calmed down. Clearing a small and humble passage through the militia, we crossed the bridge to look for a local speciality, the Juba Weaver. Somewhat uneasy as we were being watched, we failed to walk far enough up the river to find it. Unlike the lark, the weaver is real.

Later, we had compensation in the form of several new birds; our first White-tailed Swallows flew against a deep blue-black cloud, shining white below, tails flashing like beacons when they turned. Smart White-crowned Starlings strutted on the ground, while with flocks of Superb Starlings were our first Stresemann's Bush-crows. These endemic birds looked immaculate in light grey and black. Now usually treated as crows their taxonomic affinities have been unclear for years. We noticed that they were usually seen in the company of starlings. Next day we had the wonderful sight of 30 Superb Starlings, 16 White-crowned Starlings and 10 Bush-crows sitting on a flat-topped acacia. However, we had come to the end of our time in the south, and once our driver was back on some tarmac, nothing could stop him, and we flew north like the wind.

Half way back to Addis, we stayed at Awassa, by the lake. The bungalows were in a small wood, in which literally hundreds of Marabous were nesting. Walking on paths between the bungalows was hazardous, and required an umbrella. At night, however, the birds spent their time chucking down sticks and other unwanted rubbish on the tin roofs. With that, and the smell of the fish market, it was tough on the ears and nose, yet the market was very photogenic, although the locals had cottoned on to this, and we had to pay charges. There was, however, a jetty out on to the lake, which was wonderful for photography.

Once back in Addis Ababa, it became clear that our driver had seen more than enough of Ethiopia's byways, and on hearing that we were proposing to drive up a volcano, he quit. His replacement, for our journey north and east, became just as mystified by our demands, but was a bit less frantic about his – much older – vehicle.

Aloe sp.

The Ankober escarpment 26 Nov. 1995
Note Ba standing on the top!

The Blue Nile gorge at Debre Libanos is extremely impressive, as were the pink eyelids and blue buttocks of a male Gelada baboon, sitting on a cliff edge with his wives. He had huge fangs, a pink breast-patch, a lovely tawny cape, and not in the least abashed by being scrutinised at close quarters, he made no effort to move away. The cliff here was about 3000 feet high. The Gelada baboons are endemic to Ethiopia and live only on grass. As this doesn't produce much energy, they spend most of their time sitting down to eat, but they are very sociable, and rather less surprising to look at than some of their more colourful relatives.

A few days spent driving up and down escarpments, sometimes at night, had produced some interesting nightjars and we had found a rare francolin – Harwood's – one dawn on a hillside, after a particularly rocky drive. That experience was mild compared to the discomfort we later experienced in our attempt to find the Ankober Serin, a small finch which lives only at the top of the escarpment at Ankober, where the Ethiopian highlands plummet spectacularly down thousands of feet to the plains, and ultimately to the Danakil desert. That inhospitable salt pan has the distinction of dipping to the lowest point on the earth's surface, and it is hot. The people there – the Afar – used to have a curious means of welcoming strangers by cutting off their testicles. I suppose that living in a temperature of 50 degrees with no water, one would do anything for amusement.

The escarpment at Ankober (*above*). Note Barbara surveying the view.

Starspotted Nightjar - 29 November - Awash

Our approach to the escarpment was confusing. Initially we found the right road, which was rough enough, but didn't go far enough along it. Then we tried a different track, where the Toyota felt as if it was lifting its wheels individually to get over the rocks – rather like climbing the Great Pyramid on an elephant – and after some miles we gave up. Eventually we knew we were in the right place, as great swathes of cloud came boiling up and we couldn't see a thing. Everything was wet, misty and mysterious, and even standing on the edge of the cliff one could only see down a few yards. Having been assured by some locals that the cloud wouldn't lift that day, we drove to the next village, to check whether the road to our eventual destination was passable. Having lost several thousand feet in altitude, we climbed back up again the next day to look for the Ankober Serins.

I was assured later, by people who know, that we must have been within a couple of hundred yards of them, so good marks for effort. At least I drew the view.

Ethiopia never ceases to surprise. Having dropped off the highlands to drive for miles across the plains, it feels as if this flat land will go on for ever, and can't go any lower. Then one comes to the rather primitive lodge at the Awash National Park, and, amazingly, it sits on the lip of one of those gorges that suddenly appear in the plain like a great gash or subsidence, with the Awash River running far down at the bottom. The verandah of the dining room almost overhangs the cliff, and the tame Fan-tailed Ravens come onto the rail and beg for food, and then swing out over the gorge in a sweep which in six feet takes them hundreds of feet above the river. An evening drive for nightjars gave us nice views of one of the more easily identifiable of these cryptic birds, the **Star-spotted Nightjar (*far left*)**. Most of the nightjars seen on the ground are problematic, and as I know well, look nothing like their portraits in the bird guides. The song is the give-away, but usually you can't see the bird that is singing. This particular bird was quite unshy, and stayed happily while the torch shone on it for several minutes.

Exploring the almost-extinct volcano called Fantalle produced one of the dullest and rarest birds, not surprisingly called the Sombre Rock Chat. Its appearance is described in *The Birds of Africa* in one word – nondescript. I did not even draw it.

Neither was I able to draw one of the most enigmatic animals, the Somali wild ass. We had driven miles into the shimmering heat of the desert to look for this elusive species, and in this succeeded, though the animals we saw were incredibly shy, and galloped off at half a mile. They resemble zebra at a distance, grey in the haze, having a stiff up-standing mane, and in their wildness seemed to embody the very spirit of their remote, untamed environment.

A Fan-tailed Raven (*left*) perches on railings by the lodge at Awash.

Kupé:-
Rock face in the forest
near picathartes nest site

A rock-face in the forest, the site of a
nest of the Grey-necked Picathartes.

A West African mountain

During a casual conversation one day with Chris Bowden, we learned that he was in the process of organising a small party of UK ringers to spend some time on Mount Kupé, in Cameroon. At the time, Chris was living in Nyasoso, a village on the mountain, spearheading the Mount Kupé Forest Project. This aimed to encourage and inform the local people about the importance of forest conservation, particularly for the endangered Mount Kupé Bush-Shrike, using a logo of this extremely rare bird on T-shirts as a constant reminder of the significance of the mountain.

We jumped at the chance to join a ringing expedition and work in a completely novel environment, where there would be many new species. We spent a fortnight on the mountain, with a party of ten experienced ringers from organisations such as the British Trust for Ornithology and the Forestry Commission (as it was then called). Staying in the sprawling and cheerful village was fine; the slight drawback, which became apparent straight away, was that to get to the best sites for the nets, and service them, entailed a climb of about 3.000 feet, returning down at the end of the day. The descent was rather worse than the climb, which certainly left a few members of the party seriously short of breath. Not long before this trip, I had I injured a shoulder, and one day, when coming down the mountain, I was about to fall, and put out an arm to grab a root. I slipped nevertheless, and wrenched my shoulder badly, which was extremely painful. This was inconvenient, since one often had to use both arms to pull oneself up the path, and my energetic hill-climbing was slowed down somewhat.

We explored the mountain along two main paths, known as the 'shrike trail' and 'Max's trail', and another trail which meandered across the lower slopes, but did not ascend far in altitude. However, it was good birding habitat, by a stream running through a mixture of secondary vegetation, with scattered tall trees and clearings. Higher up, there was dense forest, with another stream and a waterfall, and a massive rocky outcrop. The lower section of Max's trail also ran through cultivation and secondary forest, where there were scattered trees, not very tall, with foliage starting at about 20 feet and crowns no higher than 60 feet. Much of the ground below was covered with a dense growth of coco-yam, up to a height of four feet or so. At the start of the trail, where it leaves the village, the lower storey was much denser and higher, with elephant grass ten feet high, and bananas. In general, birdlife was much more visible on both the lower sections of the trail, where there was secondary vegetation, than at higher altitudes in the primary forest.

Nets were set for the first few days in primary forest at about 3,500 feet on the shrike trail, in an area where the bush-shrike had been seen on several occasions. The weather was dry, as the rains were well over, but dense cloud would often drift slowly through the trees. The forest floor was drying out quite rapidly, and this had a marked effect on bird activity, which appeared to be minimal, with hardly any song to be heard at all. In the first three days, only one substantial bird party was seen, consisting of Grey-headed Greenbuls, Black-headed Oriole, African Paradise Flycatcher, Olive Sunbird, a woodpecker and a warbler. Going above the area where the nets were set, to around 4200 feet, there was more visible activity, and greenbuls chattered in the tree-tops.

Kype 22 November

Greynecked Rockfowl –

Bill black on upper mandible from nostril forwards –
black on lower mandible extends from sharp
point at gape around eye and ear
coverts extending in a thin line
either side over forehead

Dusky powder blue over base
of upper mandible and
bordered by black line

Dark ring around
eye, which is
huge and
luminous

Legs & feet Davy's grey – the
hind claw strongly arched, the
four claws small –

on closed wing the black
primaries show as a wedge

168

Max's trail – going up to 4,800 feet – is generally not as steep as the shrike trail, but is much longer and extremely difficult walking, so the base camp at 4,300 feet needed over an hour's scramble to reach it. There were patches of very dense shrubs, whose cut stems were apt to catch on a backpack, and force one to crawl up some stretches of path. There were also many fallen trees, some very large, and difficult to scramble over. The forest along this trail, which is on a flank of the mountain about half a mile away from the shrike trail, wears a slightly different aspect. The trees are larger and wider apart, and some of them huge, with great moss-shaggy branches and clumps of epiphytes, and the understorey in many places is quite low and not too dense. The weather became sunnier and hotter, and the forest lighter, without the drifting cloud. This, or the higher altitude, resulted in a greater degree of bird activity and noise. Because of the daily drag up the path, we decided to make a fly camp and stay for several nights. However, this meant that food and water had to be carried up from the village, and the first evening's hot meal arrived cold, and had to be heated up, with disastrous results for some stomachs.

Undoubtedly the most spectacular and iconic bird we netted on Mount Kupé was the **Grey-necked Picathartes (*left*)**. There are two closely related species of picathartes, one in Guinea and Ghana, the other occurring from Cameroon to Gabon, though their relationships to other birds are far from clear. The old names of bald-crow and rock-fowl reflect this problem, but whatever the case, they have a semi-prehistoric look about them. A long neck, long legs and bizarrely coloured bare heads, short wings and an ample tail, and a predilection for rocky ground in dense forest add up to a suite of characters designed to stir the interest of the most laid-back birder.

We had been shown a nest under an overhanging rock near a small waterfall. It looked as if it was in the process of being built, just the base of a mud cone plastered to the rock-face, though in fact I believe the birds had nested earlier, during the rains. I sat down nearby to make a detailed drawing of the nest-site, and while doing so, one of the birds called – a deep, croaking rattle from nearby in the undergrowth – and another one answered from the far side of the stream. Catching a sight of them was more difficult, and I had to make do with a brief image of one disappearing rapidly out of sight in a series of bounding hops near the waterfall. They called for ten minutes, on and off, and were in the vicinity, though calling infrequently, for at least another two hours. One bird put up from the ground about a hundred yards away flew quickly downhill, and disappeared in a second. Barbara saw another one do the same thing further along the path a little later.

Having the bird in the hand was a revelation; it was half way between holding a hare and a particularly vigorous bantam cock – a strong, wild, muscular and smooth-silhouetted creature, with long thighs, and a powerful bill. The legs and feet are well adapted to a life bouncing over rocks, for though the legs are long, the toes are rather short, and the hind claw is much longer than the front claws. The real wonder for me lay in its eyes – very large and intensely black, but also amazingly luminous, with great depths like a starlit night. I wondered how many millions of years eyes like this had been scanning the forest floor, for I couldn't help feeling that this was an ancient being from primeval forests, whose fellow forest dwellers – avian or mammalian – had long become extinct.

When the bird was released, it flew to a log, and then jumped down and leapt away on the ground, leaving me with the feeling that it had been almost impertinent to have detained something so wild and free. Restraint was in every way alien to its character – or seemed to be more so than with other birds.

Mt Kupe 27 Nov 92
Whitethroated Mountain Babbler

Bill ivory-horn, duskier round nostril and culmen
legs + feet pale grey claws ivory   Iris Davys grey + woodchat
Crown to nape deep rich maroon-chestnut, almost black
in a poor light
Call a guttural harsh babbling
Wing 117 Tarsus 34 Bill to skull 23.8 Weight 64gr

deep maroon ends here
paler loves and around base of bill
dark olive
cheeks faintly suffused warmish
Blackish very round eye

Underparts cinnamon thym a bit greyer & few fine rictal bristles

Upper tail coverts rufous rump a bit more tawny tail blackish brown

Had views of a party on moss covered branches. v active typical babbler scratchy + jumpy

A small, sociable and arboreal babbler which only occurs in Cameroon and nearby parts of Nigeria is Gilbert's (or White-throated) Mountain Babbler. It was discovered not much more than fifty years ago by the West African specialist William Serle, and named by him after his African assistant Gilbert Nkwocha, who probably first collected it. It is a striking bird, reminiscent of a dipper, though clambering around in the tree-tops, with a strikingly white face and throat set off by the rich brown of the rest of the plumage. In a good light, the top of the head is a deep maroon-chestnut, often looking almost black. At our highest camp on Kupé we had excellent views of a party foraging among mossy branches 60 or 70 feet up in a big tree. They were jumping and scrambling about, peering below twigs, flicking off little bits of moss, then suddenly bouncing up a long branch to explore another area. The white throat patch is very evident from below, though the pale eye is less easy to see. Fortunately they came down lower at times, within range of the nets, and we could examine them more closely.

Greyheaded Broadbill Kupe

Sides of breast orange whtns broad creamy central stripe extending into belly with dark sepia broad streaks bordering white centre of belly creamy white tawny whtns loves

The **Grey-headed Broadbill** (*right*) is the largest of the three species of broadbills in Africa – all of them being duller and browner than their rather gaudy relatives in the Orient – though the bright orange-rufous patches on the breast of this bird were conspicuous enough while it was in the hand.

Drawings of Gilbert's Mountain Babbler (*above*) from a netted bird in the hand.

An impression of the Grey-necked Picathartes (*left*) near its nest.

Mt Kupe 24 NOV

African Piculet

Swollen bare skin arund eye
raspberry red - eye very small
and bright red brown
dotted white line nea ear
coverts and underneath
rear g orbital area
legs & feet same colour as
orbital ring but a bit paler

African Piculets.

The piculets are tiny woodpeckers which are most diversified in South America, where there are about 27 species, all looking very similar. However, there are another three in South-east Asia, and just one in Africa. A bird three inches long, which persists in always being on the far side of a stem, is not an easy subject to draw, but this one was watched on the Nature Trail on Kupé, and then very considerately flew into the net, so some details could be added. I was struck by what a tiny eye this little bird has – a bright reddish-brown – surrounded by rather garish bare skin coloured a sort of raspberry red. One wonders just how many aeons this family of little peckers has been around, for there to be such close similarities between birds from the Amazon and the Mekong; was some ancestral piculet tapping away before the continents began to drift apart?

The **African Piculet** (*left*), though a dumpy little bird, is entertaining to watch as it forages amid the bamboo stems, moving a bit like a nuthatch in its own tiny world.

The **White-bellied Robin-Chat** (*right*) was another of those small forest birds determined not to show itself, and glimpses were too brief for making a sketch. However, when caught in the net at last, it proved to be surprisingly small, and more compact than most robin-chats; it was much more like an akalat, though with the red and black tail of its larger relatives.

The two **Fire-crested Alethes** (*overleaf*) were seen when I was coming down the mountain slowly one day on my own, and was able to watch these two birds as they investigated an ant trail. One of them jumped up onto a short, dead moss-covered stem where it could be seen well, and there were some other birds there – Brown-chested Alethes – which were pretty inconspicuous. I made a quick drawing in the notebook, and used that as the basis for this sketch as soon as I was back in camp.

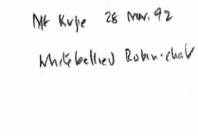

Mt Kupe   28 Nov. 92
White-bellied Robin-chat

All head olive brown with just
a hint of white feathers on
upper lores at top front edge
of eye
legs and feet grey
Eye burnt umber

wing 69
weight 15.5

Outer vane of outer feather
v. narrowly black

Fire-crested Alethes in my brein, Kope, '21 November

Fire-crested Alethes.

Postscript

Many parts of East Africa have undergone dramatic changes in the last few decades, and, in retrospect, I have been very fortunate in that my travels started nearly 50 years ago. On a recent visit I watched an otherwise insignificant event, which seemed to epitomise the passing of an era, and inspired the poem. The beauty of a sunset on Kilimanjaro will remain, though, and this ancient land has seen more changes in its time than we can imagine.

The herdsman

Remote and silent on the evening plain,
before the cold stars pierce the heated air,
a slow procession winds its dusty way.
A line of wide-horned cattle tread, heads down,
unhurriedly, into another night,
trailing a slim white echo of the dust
and glare of day.

Wind-drifted choking clouds, in red and white,
that blurred short shadows of the hot, high sun
are stayed, but now a slender shadow falls
and lengthens where the busy dust is laid.
A red-cloaked Maasai leans there on a cane,
gazing with misty red-rimmed eyes upon
that timeless scene.

To Amboseli and beyond he knows,
to hills and plains where dim clouds hang
as if to pull a dusky mantle down
upon the land. The orange flare
of dusk, that strives to live in the
cerulean sky, records the transient record of the
cattle passing by.

There comes a sudden, startling loss of light.
A silent tide of blackness runs – a dark flood
spilling from the even cone where
Meru mountain stands. Nomads of night,
cattle and herdsman are lost in shadows,
tracking a path in life as wayward as the dust
that blows.

The red cloak, stained with the changeless earth,
becomes the essence of the dying day,
for anthills and the whistling thorn
are left to catch, but not to hold, its fading
fire – stray shafts of light that burn, then cool
from red to rose, and linger last, and purest
on Kilimanjaro's snows.

175

Acknowledgments

Many people have been instrumental, even if sometimes unwittingly, in helping to bring about this book. Early mentors whose inspiration and advice – and friendship – were pivotal were Richard Richardson, and R.B. and Chloe Talbot-Kelly, and it is particularly pleasing to have the opportunity of paying a small tribute to them now.

Giants in African ornithology and natural history, at whose feet I sometimes sat at meetings of the British Ornithologists' Club, and elsewhere, included Reg Moreau, Pat Hall, Hugh Elliott, Charles Pitman, James Monk and Cyril Mackworth-Praed, who urged me to make my first trip to Africa. Latterly, Leslie Brown and Emil Urban were of course responsible for the genesis of *The Birds of Africa*, and for inviting me to contribute illustrations. Over succeeding years, it was a pleasurable, if sometimes exacting, task working with Hilary Fry and the late, and deeply lamented, Stuart Keith, and their friendship and encouragement was, quite simply, wonderful. I should also mention, in this connection, Andy Richford, for six of the seven volumes the book's godfather at Academic Press, who steered that sometimes capricious vessel of a project safely between Scylla and Charybdis and many other hazards.

The field trips in Africa were only made possible by the unstinting support of friends living there, and whose friendship and shared experiences made the whole business of working through this project a much lighter task than it would have been otherwise. Pre-eminent among these are Neil and Liz Baker, Miles and Liz Coverdale, Billy and Nancy Cooper, Alex Boswell, and Johno and the late Kimbo Beakbane. It is impossible to imagine that I could ever have done a tithe of this work without these people. I also had great help in varying capacities from Don Turner, David Pearson, Ken Newman, Alan Kemp, Simon Calburn, Reg and Barbara Weaver, the Fox family, Rudolph Schmidt, Derek Pomeroy, John Ash, John Atkins, Chris Bowden, Richard Howard, Per Hirslund and Stein Nielsen. I am also indebted to many more people for discussions or incidental assistance at various times, and if I can't remember their names, no discourtesy is intended!

I am extremely grateful to Trevor Poyser and Nigel Redman for reading the text, and making many helpful amendments and suggestions, and especially to Mark Cocker and Jonathan Elphick, whose careful reading, and advice, were invaluable. My thanks also go to Sir John Chapple, for finding the time both to read and study the book, and for his very welcome foreword. I must also pay tribute to the meticulous care which Julie Dando, of Fluke Art, took in the design and production of this book.

Finally, none of any of this could have happened without the support and encouragement at all times of my wife Barbara – and even this tribute seems hopelessly lame and inadequate, so I have dedicated the book to her, in some small recognition of all she did to make it possible.

For readers who have enjoyed this book, and would like to support the conservation of African birds and their habitats, the **African Bird Club** welcomes new members. It provides a world-wide focus for African ornithology, and publishes an excellent twice-yearly colour bulletin.

Visit the website at www.africanbirdclub.org

or write to the club c/o BirdLife International, Wellbrook Court, Girton Road, Cambridge CB3 0NA.